Anna Del Conte
Classic Italian Recipes

Anna Del Conte
Classic Italian Recipes

75 signature dishes

hamlyn

An Hachette UK Company
www.hachette.co.uk

First published in Great Britain in 2011 by
Hamlyn, a division of Octopus Publishing Group Ltd
Endeavour House
189 Shaftesbury Avenue
London
WC2H 8JY
www.octopusbooks.co.uk

ISBN 978-0-600-62178-2

A CIP catalogue record for this book is available from the British Library

Printed and bound in China

10 9 8 7 6 5 4 3 2 1

Both metric and imperial measurements are given for the recipes.
Use one set of measures only, not a mixture of both.

Ovens should be preheated to the specified temperature. If using a
fan-assisted oven, follow the manufacturer's instructions for adjusting
the time and temperature. Grills should also be preheated.

This books includes dishes made with nuts and nut derivatives.
It is advisable for those with known allergic reactions to nuts and nut
derivatives and those who may be potentially vulnerable to these
allergies, such as pregnant and nursing mothers, invalids, the elderly,
babies and children, to avoid dishes made with nuts and nut oils.
It is also prudent to check the labels of preprepared ingredients for
the possible inclusion of nut derivatives.

The Department of Health advises that eggs should not be consumed
raw. This book contains some dishes made with raw or lightly cooked
eggs. It is prudent for more vulnerable people such as pregnant and
nursing mothers, invalids, the elderly, babies and young children to
avoid uncooked or lightly cooked dishes made with eggs.

Meat and poultry should be cooked thoroughly. To test if poultry is
cooked, pierce the flesh through the thickest part with a skewer or fork
– the juices should run clear, never pink or red.

Contents

Introduction

There are 20 regions in Italy, each with its own classic recipes and within those regions are many towns and villages which all have their own classic recipes and variations.

One of my most reliable books, *La Cucina d'Oro* – an anthology compiled by the Chefs Federation and the Accademia Italiana della Cucina – lists 2,000 recipes, of which I would say around half are 'classic'. In addition, there are many variations on classic recipes. For example, spaghetti with clams can be '*al pomodoro*' – with tomatoes – or '*in bianco*' – without tomatoes. *Vitello tonnato*, a dish made with cold veal, is another recipe that has variations, both of which are considered classics. In Milan it is made without mayonnaise while in Piedmont mayonnaise is added.

So, from all these classic recipes, how could I choose only 75? I decided to use three criteria: first, I would choose dishes I enjoy cooking and eating. I cannot possibly test and taste something I am not keen on. Second, I would include recipes for which the ingredients are easily available and, more important, are good. And third, I selected the recipes I know have been most pleasing to my friends, family and many members of the public I have cooked for over the years. And, after over 40 years of writing recipes, I daresay I am quite a reliable judge.

I hope you will enjoy every recipe in this book. Individually, the recipes are full of taste and character and, as a collection, I hope they celebrate a central theme – that simplicity is the key to all Italian cooking.

Key ingredients

I feel that the appeal of Italian cooking lies in the use of ordinary ingredients, ingredients that are staples in any 21st-century larder or cupboard. Most modern cooks now have olive oil, tinned tomatoes, risotto rice, oregano, basil and lemons to hand and know the basics of how to use them.

To make an Italian dish, nobody needs to buy a long list of ingredients which will be used once and, afterwards, will clutter up the kitchen cupboard for months, or even years, until they are past their 'best before' date and you throw them out.

As examples, look at the recipes for the Milanese Veal Escalopes on page 98, Bucatini with Pancetta and Tomatoes on page 53 or Cuttlefish Stewed in Wine on page 93. These three dishes need only a few ingredients, including the main ingredient and the salt. No fusion, only the right amount of the right flavouring to enhance the basic flavour of the key ingredient of the dish.

Some ingredients you could keep to hand are:
- anchovies (fresh or preserved in salt or oil)
- capers
- a range of cheeses, such as mozzarella, Parmesan, pecorino, ricotta, fontina, Gorgonzola, dolcelatte and mascarpone
- hams, such as prosciutto crudo, parma and speck
- polenta
- pulses
- risotto rice
- tomatoes
- mushrooms
- red wine vinegar
- balsamic vinegar

Throughout the book I use unsalted butter, Italian 00 flour and sea salt, the same ingredients that are used in Italy. I use two kinds of oil: olive oil and extra virgin olive oil. For cooking I use the pure olive oil, not the extra virgin, which I keep for salads, fish and other dishes when the flavour of the oil must come through. I have specified this in every recipe and it's advisable to follow what I suggest as good ingredients are crucial to good food. It used to be that you had to go exclusively to Italian delis for good quality produce, but these days most ingredients are available from supermarkets.

8

Basic skills and recipes

Everyone should be able to create classic Italian recipes at home, whatever their skills as a chef, but throughout the book, I have highlighted some basic skills and recipes that you can go on to use for other recipes. For example, the simple bolognese sauce, with its fresh, pure ingredients, on page 62 can be adapted to use in a number of dishes and will transform them in a way that a sauce out of jar could never do. If you can find the time to make the egg pasta on page 58 then you can really create classic Italian lasagne or try making your own basic pizza dough (page 68) for homemade pizzas that are far better than shop-bought ones.

Kitchen equipment

A kitchen well stocked with chopping boards, sharp knives and a range of pans and baking tins in different sizes is really all you'll need. Be sure to have a large saucepan. You cannot cook pasta properly in a small saucepan as the pasta needs plenty of space to move around in the boiling water to stop it sticking to the bottom of the pan.

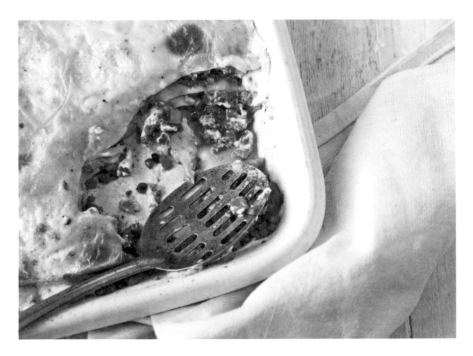

Antipasti

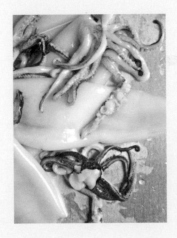

Bruschetta

MAKES 6 SLICES

loaf of coarse white
bread, such as
Pugliese

2 garlic cloves

6 tablespoons olive oil

6 ripe tomatoes

3 teaspoons wild fennel
seeds

sea salt and pepper

*The original Roman bruschetta is topped with garlic and oil.
This is a Tuscan bruschetta, made with ripe tomatoes and a
sprinkling of wild fennel seeds.*

1 Cut the bread into 6 slices, each about 15 mm (¾ inch)
thick, and score a crisscross pattern lightly across the surface
with the point of a small knife.

2 Grill the bread on both sides over charcoal or wood
embers (or under the grill) to crisp through and place
them on a dish.

3 Cut the garlic cloves in half and rub the cut sides over
the top of each piece of toast.

4 Scatter the chopped tomatoes over the toast.

5 Drizzle about 1 tablespoon oil over each one and
sprinkle over a little salt, plenty of pepper and the
fennel seeds.

Stuffed mussels
Cozze ripiene

SERVES 4

1 kg (2 lb) mussels

2 unwaxed organic lemons, cut into quarters

6 garlic cloves

125 ml (4 fl oz) olive oil

5 tablespoons chopped flat leaf parsley

5 tablespoons dried breadcrumbs

sea salt and pepper

This is the most common recipe for stuffed mussels, but there are slights variations in every region. In Emilia-Romagna, chopped mortadella and Parmesan are also added.

1 Put the mussels in a bowl of cold water and scrub them with a stiff brush. Scrape off any barnacles and use a sharp knife to remove the beards. Discard any mussel that stays open after you have tapped it against a hard surface. Rinse again in clean water.

2 Put the lemon quarters and 5 garlic cloves into a large frying pan. Add the mussels, cover and cook, shaking the pan occasionally, over a high heat until the mussels are open. Discard any mussels that remain closed.

3 Fully open the mussels and remove and discard half of each shell. Loosen the mussels on the lower half and place them on a baking sheet.

4 Strain the liquid left in the frying pan into a bowl through a muslin-lined sieve. Mix together the oil, parsley and breadcrumbs and season to taste with salt and pepper. Finely chop the remaining garlic and add to the breadcrumb mixture together with the strained liquid.

5 Place a little of the mixture over each mussel and bake in a preheated oven, 220°C (425°F), Gas Mark 7, for about 7 minutes until golden-brown.

Carpaccio

SERVES 4

300 g (10 oz) fillet of beef

1 egg yolk

180 ml (6¼ fl oz) olive oil

2 tablespoons organic lemon juice

1 teaspoon Dijon mustard

few drops of Worcestershire sauce *or* Tabasco sauce

sea salt and pepper

The original carpaccio, which was created by Giuseppe Cipriani at his Venetian restaurant Harry's Bar in 1961, was made with raw beef, as in the recipe below.

1 Cut away any skin or nodules from the beef and put it in the freezer for about 3 hours to harden (this will make it easier to slice thinly).

2 Put the egg yolk, 2 tablespoons of the oil, the lemon juice, mustard, Worcestershire or Tabasco sauce and salt and pepper in the bowl of a food processor. Process for 30 seconds, then slowly pour in the remaining oil as if you were making mayonnaise. Season to taste with salt and pepper.

3 Remove the beef from the freezer and put it on a board. Use a very sharp knife (an electric knife is ideal) to slice the meat as thinly as possible. Arrange the slices on individual plates.

4 After about 1 hour, when the meat has returned to room temperature, spoon the sauce over the slices and serve immediately.

Baked courgettes with mint and parsley
Zucchine al forno

SERVES 4

500 g (1 lb) medium
courgettes

2 tablespoons chopped
flat leaf parsley

4 tablespoons chopped
mint

2 garlic cloves, chopped

4 tablespoons dried
breadcrumbs

6 tablespoons olive oil,
plus extra for greasing

sea salt and pepper

Mint is not often used in Italy. It appears in Rome with baked artichokes and in Sardinia also with artichokes, in a lamb ragu for local pasta and in this dish.

1 Cut the courgettes in half lengthways, make some diagonal incisions on the cut sides and sprinkle the cut sides lightly with salt. Place the courgette halves on a wooden board, cut side down, for about half an hour to allow some of the liquid to drain away.

2 Put the parsley and mint in a bowl with the garlic and breadcrumbs. Gradually add half the oil, beating the mixture with a fork. Season with plenty of pepper and a little salt.

3 Wipe the courgettes with kitchen paper and lay them, cut side up, on an oiled baking sheet. Spoon a little of the herb mixture on each half and drizzle 1 tablespoon oil over the halves. Cover the courgettes with foil and bake in a preheated oven, 180°C (350°F), Gas Mark 4, for 15 minutes. Remove the foil and continue baking for about 15 minutes more or until the courgettes are tender and the tops are crisp.

4 While the courgettes are still hot drizzle over the remaining oil. Serve warm or at room temperature.

Stuffed aubergines

Melanzane ripiene alla pugliese

SERVES 4

2 aubergines, each
450–500 g (14½–16 oz)

4 tablespoons olive oil,
plus extra for greasing

1 large garlic clove,
finely chopped

½ small onion *or*
1 shallot, finely
chopped

½ celery stick, finely
chopped

225 g (7½ oz) luganega
or any spicy, coarse-
grained pure pork
continental sausage,
skinned and crumbled

30 g (1¼ oz) soft white
breadcrumbs

3 tablespoons pine nuts

2 tablespoons capers,
rinsed and dried

1 egg, lightly beaten

1 tablespoon dried
oregano

3 tablespoons grated
pecorino cheese

3 tablespoons sultanas

1 large ripe tomato

sea salt and pepper

In this recipe from Puglia, spicy sausage is added to the more usual stuffing, lending to the dish a very interesting fusion of flavours.

1 Wash and dry the aubergines. Cut them in half lengthways and use a sharp knife and then a teaspoon to scoop out most of the flesh, leaving just enough to cover the skin. Take care that you do not pierce the skin.

2 Coarsely chop the flesh and put it in a colander. Sprinkle with salt, mix well and leave to drain for about 1 hour.

3 Heat 3 tablespoons of the oil in a frying pan, add the garlic, onion or shallot and celery and cook, stirring frequently, over a low heat until soft. Add the sausage meat and cook for 20 minutes, turning frequently.

4 Meanwhile, squeeze the liquid from the aubergine pulp and dry thoroughly with kitchen paper. Add the aubergine to the pan and fry gently for a few minutes, stirring frequently. Season to taste with salt and pepper.

5 Add the breadcrumbs to the mixture in the frying pan. After 2–3 minutes mix in the pine nuts. Cook for a further 30 seconds then transfer to a bowl.

6 Add the capers, egg, oregano, pecorino and sultanas to the mixture in the bowl, season with pepper to taste and mix.

7 Pat dry the inside of the aubergine shells with kitchen paper. Lightly oil a large baking dish and arrange the shells in the dish. Fill the shells with the sausage mixture. Cut the tomato into strips and place 2–3 strips on top of each aubergine. Drizzle over the remaining oil. Add 125 ml (4 fl oz) water to the bottom of the dish, cover tightly with foil and bake in a preheated oven, 190°C (375°F), Gas Mark 5, for 20 minutes. Remove the foil and bake for a further 20 minutes.

Seafood salad
Insalata di mare

SERVES 4

500 g (1 lb) mussels

500 g (1 lb) squid, cleaned

4 tablespoons wine vinegar

1 onion, halved

2 bay leaves

225 g (7½ oz) shelled scallops

12 large raw prawns in their shells

sea salt and pepper

black olives, to garnish

SAUCE

1 garlic clove, finely chopped

3 tablespoons chopped flat leaf parsley

3 tablespoons organic lemon juice

1 dried chilli, crumbled

150 ml (¼ pint) olive oil

This dish appears on every antipasto trolley. It is made with the best and freshest fish and seafood on the market and it varies from region to region. A good selection of fish, seafood and cephalopods is essential.

1 Put the mussels in a bowl of cold water and scrub them with a stiff brush. Scrape off any barnacles and use a sharp knife to remove the beards. Discard any mussel that stays open after you have tapped it against a hard surface. Rinse again in clean water.

2 Put the mussels in a large saucepan, cover and cook over a high heat, shaking the pan from time to time, until all the mussels are open. Discard any that remain closed. Shell the mussels and transfer the meat to a bowl. Discard the shells. Strain the liquid left in the pan through a muslin-lined sieve and pour it over the mussels.

3 Cut the squid sacs into strips and the tentacles into bite-sized pieces.

4 Put about 1.5 litres (2½ pints) water in a saucepan, add 2 tablespoons of the vinegar, the onion, 1 bay leaf and a little salt and bring to the boil. Add the squid and cook over a steady simmer for 5–8 minutes, depending on their size. (Squid are cooked when they become white and lose their translucency and you can pierce them with a fork.) Remove the squid from the water with a slotted spoon, drain well and add to the bowl with the mussels.

5 Put about 500 ml (17 fl oz) water in another saucepan, add the remaining bay leaf, the remaining vinegar and some salt and bring to the boil. When the water is boiling, add the scallops. Simmer for 2 minutes after the water has returned to the boil, then remove with a slotted spoon. If the scallops are large cut them into quarters. Add them to the bowl with the mussels and squid.

6 Add the prawns to the boiling water in which the scallops were cooked. Simmer for 1 minute after the water has come back to the boil, then drain and set aside to cool.

7 Peel the prawns and, if necessary, devein them. Choose about 4 of the biggest prawns and set them aside to use for the garnish. Chop the remaining prawns and add them to the bowl.

8 Make the sauce. Mix the garlic, parsley and lemon juice together in a small bowl. Add the chilli, some black pepper and salt to taste. Add the oil, beating with a fork. Taste again and adjust the seasoning.

9 Spoon the sauce over the seafood and toss gently to coat. Pile the seafood into a large bowl or divide onto individual plates and serve garnished with the reserved prawns and black olives.

Sole in sweet-and-sour sauce

Sfogi in saor

SERVES 4

500 g (1 lb) sole fillets

plain flour

vegetable oil, for frying

4 bay leaves

1 tablespoon peppercorns

¼ teaspoon ground cinnamon

pinch of ground coriander

pinch of ground ginger

sea salt

SAOR

1 heaped tablespoon sultanas

1 tablespoon pine nuts

2 tablespoons olive oil

225 g (7½ oz) onion, thinly sliced

2 teaspoons brown sugar

125 ml (4 fl oz) dry white wine

125 ml (4 fl oz) white wine vinegar

This classic dish originated in Venice, where a similar dish is also made with fresh sardines.

1 Make the saor. Soak the sultanas in a little hot water to plump them up. Dry roast the pine nuts in a heavy-based pan until just golden; take care that they do not burn.

2 Heat the oil in a frying pan, add the onion, sugar and a pinch of salt and cook until the onion is golden. Increase the temperature, add the wine and vinegar and cook briskly, stirring, until the liquid is reduced by about half. Simmer for 10 minutes.

3 Drain the sultanas and add them to the onion together with the pine nuts. Stir to combine, then set aside.

4 Wash and dry the fish. Scatter some flour on a board and season with a little salt. Lightly coat the fish with flour.

5 Heat the oil in a wok or large frying pan. When the oil is very hot, slide in the fillets, a few at a time, and fry for about 3 minutes. Turn over the fish and fry for 2 more minutes until golden. Lift the fillets out of the oil and transfer to kitchen paper to drain.

6 When all the fillets are fried arrange them neatly on a serving plate and spoon over the saor. Sprinkle with the spices and tuck the bay leaves between the fillets. Cover the dish with clingfilm and refrigerate for at least 24 hours and up to 3 days. Bring back to room temperature before serving.

Focaccia with rosemary

SERVES 4

500 g (1 lb) Italian oo flour

1 tablespoon fine sea salt

1½ teaspoons easy-blend yeast

6 tablespoons olive oil, plus extra for greasing

needles from 2 rosemary sprigs

1 teaspoon coarse sea salt

The original focaccia originated from Genoa, where it was often covered with onions. It can also be garnished with sprigs of rosemary, shavings of soft cheese or black olives. The dough remains the same. Here is the rosemary version, which I like for its fresh, clean flavour.

1 Working either on your work surface or in a bowl, make a well in the centre of the flour and sprinkle in the fine sea salt and yeast. Add 4 tablespoons of the oil and begin to mix by drawing the flour towards the centre, adding about 300 ml (½ pint) of water as you knead. The dough should be quite damp; add more water if necessary.

2 Continue to knead for about 2 minutes, then put the dough in a lightly oiled bowl. Cover the bowl with a folded damp cloth and leave in a warm place for about 2 hours or until the dough has doubled in size.

3 Put the dough on your work surface and knock it back. Transfer the dough to a 30 x 25 cm (12 x 10 inch) baking sheet and roll and press it until it fills the sheet. Cover with a cloth and leave to rise for a further hour.

4 Preheat the oven to 240°C (475°F), Gas Mark 9.

5 Pour the remaining oil into a bowl and, beating with a fork, add 1 tablespoon warm water. Dip your fingers into the oil–water mix and press down into the focaccia to form irregular hollows in the dough. Brush the remaining oil–water mix all over the top. Sprinkle over the rosemary needles and coarse salt.

6 Reduce the oven temperature to 220°C (425°F), Gas Mark 7, and bake the focaccia for about 20 minutes or until it is golden. Turn the focaccia out on a wooden board and eat while it is still warm.

Stuffed tomatoes
Pomodori ammollicati

SERVES 3-4

6 large, round tomatoes, ripe but firm

2 tablespoons chopped flat leaf parsley

2 garlic cloves, finely chopped

1 tablespoon capers, rinsed and chopped

½ small dried chilli, chopped

4 tablespoons dried white breadcrumbs

½ tablespoon dried oregano

5 tablespoons olive oil, plus extra for greasing

sea salt and pepper

Originally from Liguria, this simple stuffing is also used for other vegetables, such as aubergines, peppers, courgettes and porcini caps.

1 Cut the tomatoes in half, remove the seeds and sprinkle with salt. Arrange them, cut side down, on a wooden board and leave to drain for about 30 minutes. Wipe the inside of each half with kitchen paper.

2 Put the parsley, garlic, capers, chilli, breadcrumbs and oregano in a bowl. Mix together well and add 4 tablespoons oil. Season to taste with salt and pepper and mix well to a paste.

3 Oil the bottom of a shallow baking dish or roasting tin and transfer the tomatoes, cut side up, to the dish.

4 Spoon a little of the breadcrumb mixture into each half tomato and drizzle over the remaining oil. Cook in a preheated oven, 180°C (350°F), Gas Mark 4, for about 30 minutes until the tomatoes are soft but still whole. Serve at room temperature.

Broad beans purée
Pure di fave

SERVES 6 – 8

1.25 kg (2½ lb) fresh broad beans *or* 500 g (1 lb) frozen broad beans

3 garlic cloves

50 g (2 oz) good-quality crustless white bread

milk

100 ml (3½ fl oz) olive oil

sea salt and pepper

crostini, to serve

This is a traditional antipasto from Pulia, where it is often served with boiled wild chicory.

1 If you are using fresh broad beans, shell them. Cook the fresh or frozen beans in a saucepan of simmering water to which you have added 1 tablespoon of salt and the garlic. When the beans are tender drain them, reserving some of the water. Leave to cool.

2 Put the bread in the bowl and add sufficient milk to cover it.

3 Peel away the outer skins of the beans and put the beans, garlic and bread and milk in a food processor or blender. Blend to make a purée, while gradually adding all but about 1 tablespoon of the oil. Taste and adjust the seasoning, adding a little of the reserved water if the mixture is too thick. It should have a soft consistency.

4 Spread the purée on crostini, moistened with the reserved oil, or serve piled in a dish surrounded by crostini.

Roasted peppers
Peperoni alla piemontese

SERVES 4

4 red or yellow peppers

6 canned anchovy
fillets, drained, *or*
3 salted anchovies,
cleaned and rinsed

3 garlic cloves

2 tablespoons chopped
flat leaf parsley

1 dried chilli, chopped

5 tablespoons olive oil

The peppers that come from the Piedmont region are large and sweet, making them perfect for roasting.

1 Hold the peppers over the flame of a burner or set them in hot charcoal and grill them all over. (Alternatively, put them under a hot grill.) When the side in contact with the heat is charred, turn the peppers until all the skin, including the top and bottom, is charred. Transfer them to a plastic bag and leave to cool.

2 Use a sharp knife to remove the skin, then cut the peppers in half and remove the stalk and seeds. Cut them lengthways into strips and arrange the pieces in a dish.

3 Put the anchovies, garlic, parsley and chilli in a mortar and pound with a pestle or chop finely and mix together.

4 Put the oil and anchovy mixture in a heavy-based frying pan and heat slowly, stirring and pounding, until the mixture is thoroughly mashed.

5 Spoon the mixture over the peppers and leave to marinate for at least 4 hours and, if time permits, for up to a week. The longer you leave them, the better the flavour.

Primi

Minestrone with pesto
Minestrone alla genovese

SERVES 6

2 litres (3½ pints) vegetable stock *or* water

150 g (5 oz) aubergines, cut into small cubes

150 g (5 oz) French beans, trimmed and broken into short pieces

200 g (7 oz) cannellini beans, cooked or canned

200 g (7 oz) potatoes, cut into small cubes

250 g (8 oz) red onion, sliced

150 g (5 oz) courgettes, cut into small cubes

200 g (7 oz) spinach beet, coarsely shredded

2 celery sticks, cut into short pieces

100 g (3½ oz) cultivated mushrooms, chopped

4 ripe tomatoes, peeled and coarsely chopped

3 garlic cloves, sliced

4 tablespoons olive oil

sea salt and pepper

150 g (5 oz) small tubular pasta, such as ditalini

6 tablespoons pesto (see pages 48–9)

grated Parmesan cheese, to serve

Minestrone is made the length and breadth of Italy. This version, which is equally good served cold, has a clean, fresh flavour.

1 Put the stock or water in a heavy-based heatproof casserole and add all the vegetables, the garlic, the oil and 2 tablespoons salt. Bring to the boil, then simmer, without boiling, uncovered, for about 1½ hours. (The longer you cook minestrone the tastier it will be.) The vegetables will not break up or become mushy during cooking. Season to taste with pepper and more salt if necessary.

2 Add the pasta to the casserole, making sure that there is enough water in the pot but bearing in mind that the soup should be thick.

3 Ladle the soup into warm serving bowls and spoon 1 tablespoon pesto into the centre of each serving. Serve with the Parmesan in a separate bowl.

Creamed fish soup
Ciuppin

SERVES 6

1 kg (2 lb) assorted fish, such as red mullet, grouper, dogfish, gurnard, roach, whiting or John Dory

100 ml (3½ fl oz) olive oil

1 large onion, sliced

1 celery stick, trimmed and chopped

1 carrot, chopped

3 garlic cloves

300 ml (½ pint) dry white wine

250 g (8 oz) can plum tomatoes with their juice

3 tablespoons chopped fresh flat leaf parsley

sea salt and pepper

Ciuppin, a fish soup from Liguria, is a smooth version of bouillabaisse. It is easier to eat because the fish is puréed after cooking, but it takes longer to prepare. Don't leave out the fish heads, which give the soup a delicious flavour.

1 Clean and wash the fish and cut into large chunks, leaving the heads on.

2 Heat 75 ml (3 fl oz) of the oil in a large saucepan, add the onion, celery, carrot and garlic and cook gently, stirring frequently, for 10 minutes. Pour over the wine and boil rapidly to reduce by half. Add the fish, mix thoroughly and fry gently for 10 minutes, turning the fish over occasionally.

3 Add 1.5 litres (2½ pints) boiling water and the tomatoes to the pan, season to taste with salt and pepper, return the soup to the boil and simmer, covered, for 20 minutes.

4 Use a slotted spoon to transfer the fish to a plate. Remove and discard the heads, backbones, fins and any other bones. Strain the stock. Put the fish and the vegetables in a food processor or blender and process to a coarse purée.

5 Reheat the stock and add the fish and vegetables purée. Mix well and check the seasoning. Add the remaining oil and parsley, stir to combine and serve.

Parmesan and egg soup

Stracciatella

SERVES 4

1 litre (1¾ pints) meat stock

4 eggs

4 tablespoons grated Parmesan cheese

1 tablespoon dried breadcrumbs

sea salt and white pepper

This soup is made throughout central Italy, but this is the basic Roman recipe. In Le Marche a little grated lemon rind and some marjoram are added.

1 Put the stock in a large saucepan and heat to simmering point.

2 Put the eggs in a bowl, beat them and add the Parmesan and breadcrumbs. Season to taste with salt and pepper.

3 Pour 1 ladleful of the boiling stock into the bowl and mix briskly with a fork. Pour the mixture slowly into the saucepan of hot stock, beating all the time with a fork. Continue beating the soup over a low heat for 3 minutes and then serve.

Risotto with mussels
Risotto con le cozze

SERVES 4

2 kg (4 lb) mussels

300 ml (½ pint) dry white wine

4 tablespoons chopped fresh flat leaf parsley

1 garlic clove, chopped

1.2 litres (2 pints) light fish *or* vegetable stock

6 tablespoons olive oil

1 medium onion, finely chopped

1 celery stick, with the leaves if possible, chopped

1 dried chilli, crumbled

350 g (11½ oz) Italian rice, preferably Arborio or Vialone Nano

sea salt and pepper

There are several recipes for risotto with mussels that can be found along the coast of northern Italy. This version is from Venice.

1 Put the mussels in a bowl of cold water and scrub them with a stiff brush. Scrape off any barnacles and remove the beards. Discard any mussel that stays open after you have tapped it against a hard surface. Rinse again in clean water.

2 Put the wine in a large frying pan, add the mussels and cover. Cook over high heat for 3–4 minutes, shaking the pan from time to time, until the mussels are open. Remove the meat from the shells, discarding the shells and any mussels that have remained closed.

3 Strain the cooking liquid through a muslin-lined sieve, pouring it slowly so that any sand will be left in the pan.

4 Set aside about 12 of the best mussels. Roughly chop the rest and put them in a bowl. Mix in the parsley and garlic.

5 Heat the stock to simmering point in a saucepan and keep it just simmering while cooking the rice.

6 Heat the oil in a separate heavy-based saucepan, add the onion and a pinch of salt and cook until soft and starting to colour. Add the celery and chilli and cook for a further 1–2 minutes. Add the rice, stir to coat with the oil and cook for 1–2 minutes until the rice is partly translucent. Pour over the mussel liquid and stir well.

7 When the liquid has been absorbed add the stock, a ladleful at a time. Stir constantly at first. When the rice is nearly cooked, mix in the chopped mussels.

8 When ready, season to taste with salt and pepper. Transfer to a heated serving dish and scatter over the reserved mussels.

Risotto with saffron
Risotto alla milanese

SERVES 4−6
AS A SIDE DISH

1.5 litres (2½ pints) beef
or chicken stock

75 g (3 oz) unsalted
butter

2 tablespoons olive oil

1 small onion, finely
chopped

400 g (13 oz) Italian rice,
preferably Carnaroli

175 ml (6 fl oz) dry
white wine

½ teaspoon powdered
saffron or saffron
strands crushed to a
powder

sea salt and pepper

75 g (3 oz) Parmesan
cheese, grated

One of the earliest risotto recipes, this originated in Milan. It is the only risotto that is served also as an accompaniment to a meat dish, Braised veal shanks with gremolata (see pages 86–7).

1 Put the stock in a saucepan. Heat it to simmering point and keep it just simmering all through the cooking of the rice.

2 Heat 60 g (2¼ oz) of the butter and the oil in a heavy-based saucepan, add the onion and cook until the onion is soft and translucent. Add the rice and stir until it is well coated with oil. Continue cooking until the rice is partly translucent.

3 Add the wine and boil for 1 minute, stirring constantly. Add 150 ml (¼ pint) of the simmering stock. Stirring constantly, cook until nearly all the stock has been absorbed and then add another ladleful of the stock. Continue cooking and adding small quantities of stock, while stirring and keeping the risotto at a steady, lively simmer. If you use up all the stock before the rice is properly cooked add a little boiling water.

4 While the rice is cooking, dissolve the saffron in a little of the hot stock. When the rice has been cooking for about 10 minutes, add the saffron mix to the pan. When the rice is al dente, taste and adjust the seasoning, as necessary.

5 Remove the pan from the heat and mix in the remaining butter and 4 tablespoons Parmesan. Cover and leave for 1–2 minutes. Give the risotto a vigorous stir and transfer to a warm serving dish. Serve immediately, with the remaining Parmesan in a separate bowl.

Risotto with sausage
Risotto con la salsiccia

SERVES 4

350 g (11½ oz) luganega sausage *or* another pure pork, coarse-grained continental sausage

2 tablespoons olive oil

6 sage leaves, torn in half

300 ml (½ pint) full-bodied red wine, such as Barbera

1.2 litres (2 pints) light meat stock

40 g (1½ oz) unsalted butter

2–3 shallots, depending on size, finely chopped

350 g (11½ oz) Italian rice, preferably Carnaroli

sea salt and pepper

grated Parmesan cheese, to serve

Allegedly this delicious recipe originates from Monza, a suburb of Milan, where the best sausage – luganega – used to be made. Luganega is often still made as a long sausage and sold by the length.

1 Skin the sausage and crumble the meat. Heat 1 tablespoon of the oil in a nonstick frying pan and add the sage. Add the sausage and fry briskly, stirring constantly, for 5 minutes.

2 Pour over half the wine, bring to the boil and cook for about 5 minutes or until the sausage meat has just lost its raw colour. Remove the sage.

3 Meanwhile, put the stock in a saucepan, heat it to simmering point and keep it just simmering all through the cooking of the rice.

4 Put the butter and remaining oil in a heavy-based saucepan, add the shallots and fry gently for about 7 minutes or until soft and translucent.

5 Add the rice to the shallots and cook for 1–2 minutes, stirring constantly, until the grains are partly translucent. Add the remaining wine and boil briskly until is has nearly all evaporated.

6 Add the stock a ladleful at a time, adding another ladleful only when the previous one has nearly all been absorbed. About 10 minutes after you started to add the stock, add the sausage and its juices to the rice. Stir well and continue cooking for about 18 minutes or until the rice is al dente. If you use up all the stock before the rice is properly cooked add a little boiling water.

7 Check the seasoning and serve immediately, with the Parmesan in a separate bowl.

Spaghetti with tomato sauce
Spaghetti al sugo

SERVES 4 – 6

4 tablespoons olive oil

1 onion, finely chopped

1 small carrot, finely chopped

1 celery stick, finely chopped

1 garlic clove, finely chopped

2 x 400 g (13 oz) cans chopped tomatoes

4 sprigs of flat leaf parsley

1 bay leaf

1 teaspoon sugar

500 g (1 lb) spaghetti or penne

grated Parmesan cheese

sea salt and pepper

The first recipe, made with canned tomatoes, gives a dense, dark tomato sauce. The second must be made with fresh, ripe tomatoes.

1 Heat the oil in a frying pan and cook the onion for 5 minutes. Add the carrot, celery and garlic and continue to fry gently for a further 10 minutes.

2 Add the tomatoes, herbs and sugar, season to taste with salt and pepper and cook, uncovered, for 40 minutes until the oil begins to separate in small droplets around the edges. Stir occasionally.

3 Remove and discard the bay leaf and parsley stalks. Transfer the sauce to a food processor or use a stick liquidizer to purée it. Return the sauce to the frying pan.

4 Cook the pasta in a large saucepan of boiling salted water. Before the pasta is cooked, gently reheat the sauce. Pour it over the drained pasta, mix thoroughly and serve with the Parmesan.

Alternative method with fresh tomato sauce

500 g (1 lb) spaghetti

5 tablespoons olive oil

1 kg (2 lb) fresh ripe tomatoes, peeled, seeded and roughly chopped

2 garlic cloves, chopped

12 fresh basil leaves *or* 1 tablespoon dried oregano

grated Parmesan cheese (optional)

sea salt and pepper

1 Cook the spaghetti in boiling salted water.

2 Meanwhile, heat the oil in a large frying pan, add the tomatoes and garlic, season to taste with salt and pepper and cook briskly for 5 minutes, stirring frequently. Taste and adjust the seasoning.

3 Drain the spaghetti and transfer it to the frying pan. Add the basil or oregano and stir-fry for 2 minutes. Serve immediately with the Parmesan, if liked, in a separate bowl.

Spaghetti alla carbonara

SERVES 4

2 tablespoons olive oil

6 sage leaves, roughly torn (optional)

2 garlic cloves, lightly crushed

150 g (5 oz) smoked pancetta, cubed

400 g (13 oz) spaghetti

2 whole eggs and 1 egg yolk

8 tablespoons grated Parmesan cheese, plus extra to serve (optional)

60 g (2¼ oz) unsalted butter

sea salt and pepper

This dish is attributed to the carbonari (charcoal burners) who worked in the mountain forests of Lazio. The sauce became popular outside Italy after the Second World War thanks to the Allied forces in Rome, who found in the dish their two favourite ingredients: bacon and eggs.

1 Heat the oil in a large, heavy-based frying pan and add the sage and garlic. Add the pancetta and fry over a high heat until the pancetta is golden-brown and the fat has partly run out. Remove and discard the garlic.

2 Cook the spaghetti in a large saucepan of boiling salted water.

3 Meanwhile, beat the eggs in a bowl together with the Parmesan and plenty of pepper.

4 Drain the spaghetti, reserving some of the cooking water. Return the spaghetti to the saucepan, mix in the butter and then transfer to the frying pan containing the pancetta. Stir-fry for a few minutes.

5 Remove the pan from the heat and transfer the pasta to a warm bowl. Mix in the egg and Parmesan and pour over 3–4 tablespoons of the reserved water; the sauce should be fairly fluid. Mix well and serve immediately with more Parmesan on the side, if liked.

Trofie with pesto

SERVES 4

PESTO
50 g (2 oz) basil leaves
2 garlic cloves
2 tablespoons pine nuts
40 g (1½ oz) grated
  Parmesan cheese
2 tablespoons grated
  mature pecorino
  cheese
100 ml (3½ fl oz) olive oil
30 g (1¼ oz) unsalted
  butter
sea salt and black
  pepper

400 g (13 oz) trofie *or*
  other pasta

Trofie is a corkscrew-shaped pasta that is often eaten in Liguria with pesto, but pesto is good with any pasta, from spaghetti to small lasagne.

1 To make the pesto with a pestle and mortar, put the basil, whole garlic cloves, pine nuts and a pinch of salt in a mortar and grind until the mixture is a paste. Add the grated cheeses and blend thoroughly. Add the oil a little at a time, stirring with a wooden spoon. When all the oil has been added taste and adjust the seasonings.

2 To make the pesto in a blender or food processor put the basil, garlic, pine nuts, salt, pepper and olive oil in a blender and mix at high speed. Blend until very creamy. Transfer to a bowl, taste and adjust the seasoning. Mix thoroughly.

3 Spoon the pesto into a large serving bowl and add the butter. Put the bowl into a warm oven.

4 Cook the pasta in a large saucepan of boiling salted water. Drain, reserving a little of the water. Turn the trofie into the bowl and mix thoroughly with the pesto, adding 2–3 tablespoons of the pasta water if necessary to make a smooth sauce.

Spaghetti alla puttanesca

SERVES 4

500 g (1 lb) fresh ripe
tomatoes, peeled,
deseeded and roughly
chopped, or 400 g
(13 oz) can peeled
tomatoes, roughly
chopped

6 tablespoons olive oil

400 g (13 oz) spaghetti

1–2 dried chillies (to
taste), deseeded and
chopped

4 salted anchovies,
cleaned, rinsed and
chopped, or 8 anchovy
fillets, drained and
chopped

3 garlic cloves, chopped

100 g (3½ oz) pitted
black olives, sliced

1 tablespoon capers

2 tablespoons chopped
flat leaf parsley

sea salt

*This is an old recipe from the poorest district of Rome, the
Trastevere, the traditional haunt of the Roman puttane (prostitutes).
Its name derives from the fact that it is a hot sauce, quickly made.*

1 If you are using fresh tomatoes, fry them in a saucepan
with ½ tablespoon of the oil for 5 minutes. If you are using
canned tomatoes fry them for only 3 minutes.

2 Cook the spaghetti in a large saucepan of boiling
salted water.

3 Meanwhile, heat the remaining oil in a large frying pan,
add the chilli, anchovies and garlic and fry gently for
2 minutes, mashing the anchovies to a paste with a fork.
Spoon in the tomatoes and add the olives and capers.
Cook for 2 minutes.

4 When the spaghetti is cooked, drain it and turn it
immediately into the frying pan. Stir-fry for 2 minutes,
sprinkle with parsley and serve immediately.

Bucatini with pancetta and tomatoes
Bucatini all'amatriciana

SERVES 4

3 tablespoons olive oil

250 g (8 oz) unsmoked pancetta, cubed

1 small onion, finely chopped

400 g (13 oz) ripe plum tomatoes, peeled and coarsely chopped

1–2 dried chillies (to taste), chopped

400 g (13 oz) bucatini

6 tablespoons grated mature pecorino cheese

Bucatini are thick spaghetti with a hole in the middle. Spaghetti or linguine could be used as an alternative. The traditional meat included in this sauce from Amatrice, a town in the central Apennines, is pork jowl. Pancetta is a good alternative.

1 Heat 1 tablespoon of the oil in a frying pan and cook the pancetta until crisp. Use a slotted spoon or fish slice to transfer it to a large bowl and keep it warm in a low oven.

2 Put the remaining oil in the same frying pan, add the onion and fry for about 5 minutes or until soft but not coloured. Add the tomatoes and chilli and continue cooking over a moderate heat for 10 minutes.

3 Meanwhile, cook the bucatini in a large saucepan of boiling salted water. Drain and turn into the bowl with the pancetta. Stir in the tomato mixture and then the pecorino. Serve immediately.

Orecchiette with cauliflower
Orecchiette con le cime di rapa

SERVES 4

1 cauliflower, about 500 g (1 lb)

2 tablespoons pine nuts

400 g (13 oz) orecchiette

6 tablespoons olive oil

2 garlic cloves, chopped

1–2 dried chillies (to taste), deseeded and chopped

3 salted anchovies, cleaned, rinsed and chopped, *or* 6 anchovy fillets, drained and chopped

6 tablespoons grated matured pecorino cheese

sea salt

Orecchiette is a type of pasta from Pulia, where it is made with durum wheat, semolina and water. The sauce is usually made with turnip tops, which are very rarely available; cauliflower or sprouting broccoli are good substitutes.

1 Cut the cauliflower in half and divide it into small florets. Cut the stalks into small pieces. Wash and drain.

2 Bring a large saucepan of water to the boil and add 2 tablespoons salt and the cauliflower. Cook until just tender. (This will depend of the age and quality of the vegetable.) Test the thickest part of the stalk with the point of a small knife. Lift the florets and stalks out of the water and put them in a colander.

3 Meanwhile, dry-fry the pine nuts in a small, heavy-based frying pan until just golden.

4 Add the orecchiette to the boiling water and cook.

5 Heat half the oil in a large, heavy-based frying pan, add the garlic, chilli and anchovies and cook for 2–3 minutes, mashing the anchovies with a fork. Add the drained cauliflower and pine nuts and mix thoroughly.

6 Drain and pasta and turn into the frying pan. Mix thoroughly and cook for a further 2–3 minutes. Turn off the heat, mix in the remaining oil and the pecorino and serve immediately.

Pasta and cannellini beans

Pasta e fagioli alla napoletana

SERVES 4

175 g (6 oz) cannellini
beans

4 tablespoons olive oil

1 garlic clove, chopped

1 fresh red chilli,
dseeded and chopped

400 g (13 oz) can
chopped peeled
tomatoes

2 tablespoons chopped
flat leaf parsley

100 g (3½ oz) small
pasta

sea salt and pepper

Almost every region of Italy has a recipe for pasta e fagioli, *made with local beans and whatever pasta is in the larder. This is the recipe from Naples.*

1 Soak the beans in cold water overnight. The next day rinse and drain them.

2 Heat the oil in a heatproof casserole, add the garlic and chilli and fry for 1–2 minutes. Add the tomatoes and continue frying for a further 5 minutes.

3 Add the beans and fry for 3–4 minutes, stirring the whole time. Add 1.8 litres (3 pints) water to the casserole and bring to the boil. Simmer, covered, over the lowest heat for about 1½ hours or until the beans are tender.

4 When the beans are tender, season with salt and a little pepper and add half the parsley and the pasta. Cook until the pasta is ready and ladle into soup bowls. Sprinkle with the remaining parsley and serve immediately.

Spaghetti and clams in white wine
Spaghetti in bianco con le vongole

SERVES 4
1 kg (2 lb) clams
100 ml (3½ fl oz) dry white wine
400 g (13 oz) spaghetti
5 tablespoons olive oil
2 garlic cloves, finely chopped
bunch of flat leaf parsley, chopped
1 small dried chilli, deseeded and chopped

This is the Neapolitan version of this familiar dish, and it is made without tomatoes. The clams used are palourdes (carpet shells), which are more highly prized than other types.

1 Put the clams in a bowl of cold water and, if they are dirty, scrub them with a hard brush. Leave them in the water for about 20 minutes to disgorge any sand. Discard any clam that remains open after being tapped on a hard surface. Change the water and rinse again.

2 Put the wine in a large frying pan, add the clams, cover with a lid and cook over a high heat for 3–4 minutes, shaking the pan from time to time. When the clams are open, set aside about 20 of the largest. Remove the meat from the shells of the remaining clams. Discard the shells.

3 If there is sand in the bottom of the pan, strain the cooking liquid through a muslin-lined sieve and then return it to the pan. If the liquid looks clean, pour it gently into the pan. Cook the liquid over a high heat to reduce, then transfer it to a bowl.

4 Cook the spaghetti in a large saucepan of boiling salted water.

5 Meanwhile, heat the oil in the same frying pan and cook the garlic, parsley and chilli for 2 minutes. When the spaghetti is cooked, drain it and turn it into the pan. Add the clam juices and stir-fry for 1 minute.

6 Add the clams without the shells and stir-fry for 2 minutes. Transfer the spaghetti to 4 individual plates and scatter a few of the reserved clams in their shells over each serving.

Home made egg pasta by machine
La sfoglia

MAKES 400 G
(10 OZ) PASTA

300 g (10 oz) Italian 00 flour

3 eggs

This recipe is for the home made pasta of Emilia-Romagna, made with soft wheat flour (Italian 00) and eggs. Home made pasta is far superior to shop-bought fresh pasta. If you cannot make your own pasta, buy dried egg pasta of a good Italian brand, not fresh pasta made outside Italy. For the lasagne recipe on page 63, reduce the quantities to 200 g (7 oz) Italian 00 flour and 2 eggs.

1 Put most of the flour in a mound on the work surface, leaving the rest on a plate. Make a well in the centre and break the eggs into it. Lightly beat them together with a fork and then draw the flour in gradually from the inner wall of the well.

2 When the eggs are no longer runny, draw in enough flour to enable you to knead the dough. At this stage you might have to add some of the flour you set aside and even a little more from the bag. You should add enough flour for the dough to be no longer sticky. Work into a messy ball and then wash your hands and clean your work surface.

3 Knead the dough by pressing and pushing it with the heels of your hands, folding the dough, giving it a half a turn and repeating this movement for about 2 minutes.

4 Wrap the dough in clingfilm and leave to rest for at least 30 minutes before you use it.

5 Unwrap the dough and lightly dust the work surface with flour. Divide the dough into 3 portions and work on one portion at a time, keeping the remaining dough covered with a damp tea towel to prevent it from drying out.

6 To roll out the dough, set the rollers of the machine to the widest opening. Flatten one portion of dough slightly, so that it is nearly as wide as the rollers, then run the

dough through the rollers 6–7 times, folding the sheet in half and turning it through 180 degrees each time. This folding and turning is important for a smooth result. If the dough is sticky, dust it lightly with some flour.

7 Run the unfolded sheet once through each setting, closing the rollers one notch at a time until you have reached the desired thickness.

For ravioli, roll out the dough to the last setting. Cover the strips with a damp tea towel and proceed immediately as in the recipe on pages 60–1.

For tagliatelle, roll out the dough to the last-but-one setting, lay the sheets on clean tea towels letting about ⅓ of their length hang down over the end of the work surface. Turn each sheet over after 20–30 minutes, depending on the temperature and humidity of the room. The pasta is ready when it is dry to the touch and slightly leathery but still pliable. Feed each sheet through the broad cutter of the machine and lay the pasta back on the tea towels ready for cooking, as in the recipe on page 62.

For lasagne, roll out the dough to the last setting, then cut each sheet of pasta into about 20 cm- (8 inch-) lengths. Proceed immediately, as in the recipe on page 63.

8 If you have any pasta left over cut it into small squares – it does not matter if they are of different sizes – and use them in soups.

Ravioli Milanese style
Ravioli alla milanese

SERVES 4

75 g (3 oz) unsalted butter

75 g (3 oz) unsmoked pancetta, finely chopped

350 g (11½ oz) lean minced beef

150 ml (¼ pint) meat stock

1 sprig of rosemary

100 g (3½ oz) grated Parmesan cheese

1 egg

pinch of ground cinnamon

pasta made with 300 g (10 oz) Italian oo flour and 3 eggs (see pages 58–9)

1 tablespoon vegetable oil

5 sage leaves, slightly crushed

1 garlic clove

sea salt and pepper

Ravioli is made in many parts of northern Italy. This version, which is filled with meat, comes from Milan and is traditionally prepared for carnival.

1 Make the stuffing. Heat 15 g (½ oz) butter in a heavy-based saucepan. Add the pancetta and meat and fry for about 5 minutes until brown, turning the meat over frequently. Add the stock, rosemary, salt and pepper and simmer gently for 20 minutes, stirring frequently, until tender. Discard the sprig of rosemary. Transfer the meat into a bowl and leave to cool. Add 50 g (2 oz) of the Parmesan, the egg and cinnamon and mix well.

2 Make the pasta (see pages 58–9). Work on one strip of dough at the time, leaving the remaining strips covered with a tea towel. Place little mounds of the filling (about ½ teaspoon) in a straight line along the length of the strip of pasta, spacing them about 4 cm (1½ inches) apart and 3 cm (1¼ inches) from the edge. Fold the strip lengthways over the filling and use a pastry wheel to trim the edges where they meet. Use the pastry wheel to cut between each mound of filling and separate the squares. Repeat until all the ingredients have been used. If the edges do not stick together well, pinch them together lightly with moistened fingertips.

3 Drop the ravioli into a large saucepan of boiling salted water to which you have added the vegetable oil. Cover the saucepan and quickly return the water to the boil. Uncover and cook for 4–5 minutes.

4 Meanwhile, melt the remaining butter in a small saucepan. Add the sage leaves and the whole garlic clove.

Stir for 1 minute, discard the garlic (if liked) and pour the butter sauce into a warm serving bowl, Add the remaining Parmesan and keep warm in a low oven.

5 Drain the ravioli and turn them into the serving bowl. Toss them quickly but gently in the butter sauce and serve immediately.

Tagliatelle alla bolognese

SERVES 4

TAGLIATELLE

tagliatelle made with
300 g (10 oz) Italian 00
flour and 3 eggs (see
pages 58–9) *or* 300 g
(10 oz) dried egg
tagliatelle

BOLOGNESE SAUCE

30 g (1¼ oz) unsalted
butter

3 tablespoons olive oil

1 onion, chopped

50 g (2 oz) unsmoked
pancetta, cubed

200 g (7 oz) minced beef

200 g (7 oz) minced pork

1 celery stick, chopped

1 carrot, chopped

1 garlic clove, chopped

1 bay leaf

250 ml (8 fl oz) red wine

400 g (13 oz) can
chopped tomatoes

generous grating of
nutmeg

full-fat milk

sea salt and pepper

grated Parmesan
cheese, to serve

1 Make the tagliatelle (see pages 58–9).

2 Make the sauce. Heat the butter and oil in a large,
heavy-based saucepan, add the onion and cook for
5 minutes. Add the meat and fry over a high heat
for 5 minutes, breaking it up and stirring with a fork.

3 Add the celery, carrot, garlic and bay leaf and cook for
a further 17 minutes. Pour in the wine and cook over a
high heat for 2–3 minutes until it evaporates. Add the
tomatoes and bring to the boil. Season to taste with
nutmeg, salt and pepper and cook over a low heat for
2–2½ hours. Whenever the sauce gets too dry add
2–3 tablespoons milk.

4 Cook the tagliatelle in a large saucepan of boiling salted
water; fresh pasta takes only about 2 minutes to cook.
Drain but reserve some of the pasta water.

5 Spoon a few tablespoons of the sauce into a heated
bowl and add about half the pasta. Spoon more sauce over
and mix thoroughly. Add the remaining pasta and sauce.
Mix thoroughly, adding 2–3 tablespoons of the pasta
water. Serve with the Parmesan in a separate bowl.

Baked lasagne
Lasagne al forno

SERVES 4

Bolognese Sauce (see page 62)

lasagne made with 200 g (7 oz) Italian oo flour and 2 eggs (see pages 58–9)

1 tablespoon vegetable oil

1 tablespoon sea salt

75 g (3 oz) Parmesan cheese, grated

20 g (¾ oz) unsalted butter, plus extra for greasing

BÉCHAMEL SAUCE

750 ml (1¼ pints) full-fat milk

75 g (3 oz) unsalted butter

60 g (2¼ oz) Italian oo flour

generous grating of nutmeg

This great dish from Bologna is often made with green home-made pasta, which containins spinach. The recipe here is for the more common pasta used also for tagliatelle and ravioli.

1 Make the Bolognese Sauce (see page 62) and keep warm, then make the lasagne sheets (see pages 58–9).

2 Fill a large saucepan with water and add the oil and salt. Bring the water to the boil, slide in 5–6 pasta squares at a time, moving them around with a wooden spoon to stop them sticking to each other. After about 1 minute remove them with a fish slice and transfer to a bowl of cold water to rinse the starch out. Lift them out and lay them on some clean tea towels. Pat them with kitchen paper.

3 Make the béchamel sauce. Put the milk in a heavy-based saucepan and heat until very hot but not boiling. Set aside. Melt the butter in another saucepan. Draw the pan off the heat and beat in the flour. Return the pan to the heat and cook, stirring constantly, for about 30 seconds. Draw the pan off the heat and gradually pour in the milk, stirring constantly. When all the milk has been added, return the pan to the heat again and cook slowly until the sauce begins to boils. Season with salt, pepper and nutmeg and cook gently for 10 minutes, stirring frequently.

5 Butter a 20 x 30 cm (8 x 12 inch) ovenproof dish. Spread 2 or 3 tablespoons of the Bolognese sauce over the bottom and cover with a layer of lasagne set across the dish. Spread over 2 tablespoons of the Bolognese sauce and 2 tablespoons of the béchamel sauce. Sprinkle with Parmesan. Repeat the layers, finishing with a layer of béchamel sauce. Dot with the butter and cook in a preheated oven, 180°C (350°F), Gas Mark 4, for 20 minutes. Allow to rest for 5 minutes before serving.

Potato gnocchi
Gnocchi di patate

SERVES 4

1 kg (2 lb) floury potatoes, such as Desiree or King Edward

275 g (9 oz) Italian oo flour

1 teaspoon baking powder

75 g (3 oz) grated Parmesan cheese, to serve

DRESSING

75 g (3 oz) unsalted butter

2 garlic cloves, lightly crushed

6 sage leaves, torn into small pieces

Gnocchi's success lies in the variety of the potatoes used. They must be floury, and a little baking powder will make them lighter. Gnocchi are delicious dressed with butter and cheese (see below) or with a simple tomato sauce (see page 46), a few tablespoons of pesto (see page 48) or some Gorgonzola cheese melted in butter.

1 Boil the potatoes in their skins until they are just soft. Drain them and, as soon as you can hold them, peel them and purée them through a food mill or a potato ricer straight on to your work surface. (A food processor will make them gluey.) Sieve the baking powder into the flour.

2 Let the potatoes cool a little and add about three-quarters of the flour. Knead to a soft, smooth and still slightly sticky dough. Add more flour if necessary, but the less flour you add, the better the gnocchi will be. Roll pieces of dough into thin sausages and cut these into slices about 3 cm (1¼ inches) long.

3 Lightly press each gnocco against the tines of a fork and then place them on a clean tea towel. (The grooves help the gnocchi hold more sauce when they are dressed.)

4 Bring a large saucepan of salted water to the boil. Drop the gnocchi in the water in 2–3 batches. The gnocchi will sink to the bottom of the pan and then rise to the surface. Leave them for about 30 seconds, lift them out with a slotted spoon and put them in a dish. Pat them dry with kitchen paper and keep warm.

5 Heat the butter, garlic and sage for the dressing in a small saucepan until the butter is golden. Remove the garlic and pour a little sauce over each batch of gnocchi. Spoon any remaining sauce over and serve with the Parmesan.

Pizza dough

SERVES 2−3

15 g (½ oz) fresh yeast *or*
1½ teaspoons dried
yeast with ½ teaspoon
caster sugar

200 g (7 oz) bread flour

1 tablespoon olive oil

1 teaspoon sea salt

Although pizzas are rarely eaten in Italian homes – they are usually eaten at pizzerias – a good pizza topped with tomatoes and dressed with fruity olive oil and other traditional ingredients is one of the great dishes of Neapolitan cuisine. Use well-flavoured tomatoes or Fresh tomato sauce (see page 46).

1 Blend the fresh yeast in 100 ml (3½ fl oz) warm water. If you are using dried yeast, dissolve the sugar in the same amount of water, sprinkle the yeast over and leave for about 15 minutes or until frothy.

2 Put the flour on a work surface, make a well in the centre and pour in the dissolved yeast, oil and salt. Work the flour with your hands to form a smooth ball. Knead until the dough is smooth and elastic but not sticky.

3 Transfer the dough to a lightly floured bowl and cover with a damp cloth. Leave the bowl in a warm place for 1½ –2 hours or until the dough has doubled in size.

4 Once the dough has risen, knock it back and then knead it again into a ball. Leave it to rest for a further 10–15 minutes, still covered with the damp cloth.

5 Roll out the dough to a round about 25 cm (10 inches) across. Transfer the dough to a lightly floured baking sheet. With your fingers, make a slightly thicker outer edge about 2 cm (¾ inch) deep. Now the pizza is ready to be covered with the topping.

Pizza Margherita

SERVES 2

about 200 g (7 fl oz)
buffalo mozzarella

5 tablespoons olive oil

pizza dough (see
page 68)

300 g (10 oz) ripe
tomatoes, peeled and
coarsely chopped

12 basil leaves, torn

2 tablespoon grated
Parmesan cheese

sea salt and pepper

When Queen Margherita of Italy visited Naples at the end of the 19th century, a new pizza was created in her honour. The topping has the 3 colours of the Italian flag: green (basil), white (mozzarella) and red (tomato).

1   Grate the mozzarella coarsely into a bowl and add 3 tablespoons of the olive oil. Leave to stand for at least 1 hour.

2   Spread the mozzarella and its oil over the pizza base. Scatter over the tomatoes and basil and then sprinkle with the Parmesan and salt and pepper. Drizzle over the remaining oil.

3   Bake in a preheated oven, 220°C (425°F), Gas Mark 7, for about 20 minutes or until the edge of the pizza is crusty and golden-brown.

Pizza napoletana

SERVES 2

pizza dough
(see page 68)

400 g (13 oz) tomatoes,
peeled and thinly
sliced

3 garlic cloves, finely
sliced

2 teaspoons dried
oregano

2 anchovies, cleaned
and rinsed *or* 4
anchovy fillets,
drained and cut into
small pieces

1 tablespoon capers

12 pitted black olives

3 tablespoons olive oil

sea salt and pepper

This is the original pizza, created in the streets of Naples when tomatoes began to be popular. It is the simplest and, with good tomatoes, the best.

1 Spread the tomatoes and sprinkle the garlic, oregano, anchovies, capers and olives evenly over the top of the pizza base. Sprinkle with a little salt and a generous grinding of pepper and drizzle over the oil.

2 Bake in a preheated oven, 220°C (425°F), Gas Mark 7, for about 20 minutes or until the edge of the pizza is crusty and golden-brown.

Basic polenta

SERVES 4

300 g (10 oz) polenta
   bramata (coarse
   grain)

2 teaspoons sea salt

*This is the recipe for making old-fashioned polenta. Nowadays,
the most readily available polenta flour on the market is precooked,
which saves time and labour, but the results are not as good. This
soft polenta is the accompaniment to Beef Braised in Barolo Wine
(see pages 76–7), Beef braised in milk and vinegar (see page 94),
Cuttlefish stewed in wine (see pages 92–3) and many other
meat and fish dishes.*

1 Put 1.8 litres (3 pints) water in a heavy-based heatproof
casserole and bring to the boil. Add the salt and then turn
the heat down to low.

2 Add the polenta in a thin stream, stirring constantly.
If you like, add it through a funnel so that it falls slowly
into the boiling water. Stop every so often to stir the polenta
with a long wooden spoon to prevent lumps from forming.

3 When all the polenta has been added, cook over a lively
heat for 30–40 minutes. The experts say you should stir the
whole time; I have a rest every now and then.

Polenta baked in the oven
Polenta al forno

SERVES 4

300 g (10 oz) polenta
   bramata (coarse
   grain)
2 teaspoons sea salt
butter, for greasing

This is a labour- free method for making polenta with old-fashioned maize flour, not the pre-cooked sort. The result is excellent.

1 Put 1.8 litres (3 pints) water in a heavy-based heatproof casserole and bring to the boil. Add the salt and then turn the heat down to low.

2 Add the polenta in a thin stream, stirring constantly. If you like, add it through a funnel so that it falls slowly into the boiling water. Stop every so often to stir the polenta with a long wooden spoon to prevent lumps from forming. Boil the polenta for 5 minutes, stirring constantly.

3 Generously butter an ovenproof dish and spoon the polenta into it. Cover with a piece of buttered foil and cook in a preheated oven, 190°C (375°F), Gas Mark 5, for 1 hour.

Grilled polenta

SERVES 4

300 g (10 oz) polenta
   bramata (coarse
   grain)
2 teaspoons sea salt
olive oil, for brushing

This type of polenta is often served with roast chicken or rabbit or with fried fish.

1 Prepare the polenta as described opposite or in the recipe above. Using a spatula moistened with hot water, spread the hot polenta on a wooden board until it is about 3 cm (1¼ inches) thick. Leave it to cool completely, which will take about 2 hours.

2 Cut the cold polenta into squares, brush with oil and cook under a hot grill until lightly charred. Alternatively, fry the squares in olive oil.

Secondi

Beef braised in Barolo wine

Brasato al Barolo

SERVES 6

1.5 kg braising steak or brisket in a single piece

1 bottle of Barolo wine

4 tablespoons olive oil

25 g (1 oz) unsalted butter

1 onion, chopped

3 garlic cloves, chopped

2 anchovy fillets, chopped

2 tablespoons chopped flat leaf parsley

2 tablespoons chopped celery leaves

6 sage leaves, chopped

2 heaped tablespoons light brown sugar

sea salt and pepper

MARINADE

2 onions, chopped

2 carrots, chopped

2 celery sticks, chopped

3 cloves

10 juniper berries

6 black peppercorns

sprig of sage

sprig of thyme

If you don't want to open a bottle of Barolo for cooking, use another good-quality, full-bodied red wine. Polenta (see pages 72–3) is the traditional accompaniment for this dish.

1 Make the marinade. Mix together all the ingredients in a non-metallic bowl. Place the meat on top and pour over half the wine. Leave to marinate in a cool place for 24 hours, turning the meat over as often as you can remember.

2 Remove the meat from the marinade and dry it thoroughly with kitchen paper. If necessary, tie it up with kitchen string to make a neat oblong. Season to taste with salt and pepper.

3 Heat 2 tablespoons of the oil in a frying pan, add the meat and brown well all over. Transfer to a plate.

4 Strain the marinade into the frying pan and deglaze for 2 minutes, scraping up the bits at the bottom of the pan. Set aside. Discard the marinade vegetables.

5 Heat the remaining oil and half the butter in a casserole, add the onion, garlic, anchovies, parsley, sage and celery and cook, stirring frequently, for about 7 minutes. Put the meat on the vegetables, add the strained marinade liquid and the remaining wine, cover the casserole and cook in a preheated oven, 160°C (325°F), Gas Mark 3, for 1½ hours, turning the meat 2–3 times during the cooking. Sprinkle with the sugar and continue cooking for a further 1½ hours until the meat is tender. Transfer the meat to a board and cover loosely with foil.

6 Spoon all the vegetables and cooking juices into a food processor or blender and process to make a purée.

7 Return the purée to the casserole. Cook over a low heat, adding the remaining butter, little by little, while stirring well. Check the seasoning.

8 Carve the meat into slices about 1 cm (½ inch) thick, spoon some of the sauce around the slices and serve immediately.

Stuffed squid
Calamari ripieni

SERVES 4

4 large squid

4 tablespoons cooked rice

4 tablespoons olive oil

3 tablespoons chopped flat leaf parsley

1 garlic clove, finely chopped

1 small dried chilli, chopped

100 ml (3½ fl oz) white dry wine

sea salt and pepper

In some regions, breadcrumbs are used instead of the rice. The same recipe is used also to stuff cuttlefish.

1 Ask your fishmonger to clean the squid, to remove the bone and to peel off the membrane on the sac. Thoroughly wash the tentacles and the sacs.

2 Finely chop the squid tentacles, put them in a bowl and add the rice, 2 tablespoons of the oil, the parsley, garlic and chilli. Mix thoroughly and season to taste with salt and plenty of pepper.

3 Fill each sac with the rice and tentacle mixture, taking care that you do not pack the stuffing too tightly or the sac will burst during the cooking. Hold the openings together with cocktail sticks.

4 Lay the stuffed squid snugly in a single layer in a shallow, ovenproof dish. Mix together the wine and remaining oil and pour it over the squid. Bake uncovered in a preheated oven, 180°C (350°F), Gas Mark 4, for about 40 minutes or until the squid can be easily pierced with a fork, basting every 15 minutes or so. Remove the cocktail sticks before serving.

Pork braised in milk
Maiale al latte

SERVES 6

1.2–1.5 kg (2½–3 lb) rib or leg of pork

about 500 ml (17 fl oz) dry white wine

2 tablespoons olive oil

15 g (½ oz) unsalted butter

1 sprig of rosemary

1 sprig of sage

500 ml (17 fl oz) full-fat milk

sea salt and pepper

This delicious dish is traditionally claimed by two regions: Veneto and Emilia-Romagna.

1 Ask your butcher to bone, roll and neatly tie the pork and to give you the bones.

2 Put the pork in a non-metallic bowl, cover with the wine and leave overnight or even for 24 hours.

3 Heat the oil and butter in a heatproof casserole. Dry the meat with kitchen paper and place in the casserole. Fry it on all sides and the two ends. Add the herbs, as many bones as will fit in (they will make the cooking juices more flavourful) and season to taste with salt and pepper.

4 Heat the milk and slowly pour about 400 ml (14 fl oz) into the casserole. Cover the casserole, leaving the lid slightly askew to let some of the steam out, and simmer over a low heat for about 3 hours. Turn the meat 2–3 times during the cooking and check that there is enough liquid, if necessary adding more of the remaining milk.

5 When the meat is very tender and the milk in the pot has thickened and turned into dark clumps, lift it out and place on a carving board. Cover with foil to keep warm.

6 Make the sauce. Remove and discard the bones and herbs from the casserole. Skim off most of the fat from the surface of the liquid juices and add 3–4 tablespoons hot water. Boil briskly, while scraping and loosening the residues at the bottom of the casserole with a metal spoon. Taste and adjust the seasoning.

7 Remove the string, carve the pork into thin slices and arrange them on a heated dish. Spoon the cooking juices over and around the meat and serve with mashed potato.

Steamed sea bass with salsa verde
Brancino a vapore con salsa verde

SERVES 4

250 ml (8 fl oz) dry
white wine

1 onion, chopped

1 carrot, chopped

1 celery stick, chopped

2 garlic cloves

2 bay leaves

a few sprigs of flat leaf
parsley

the outside leaves of
a lettuce

1 sea bass, about 1 kg
(2 lb), cleaned but with
head and scales on

1 tablespoon olive oil

sea salt and pepper

SALSA VERDE

1 garlic clove, chopped

large bunch of flat leaf
parsley, stalks
removed and leaves
chopped

2 tablespoons capers

150 ml (¼ pint) extra
virgin olive oil

juice of 1 unwaxed
organic lemon
(to taste)

sea salt and pepper

Any large fish, such as hake, can be cooked in this way and served with salsa verde, which is one of the few sauces that is not for dressing pasta. It is a versatile sauce, ideal for boiled or roasted fish and for boiled meat or fowl or vegetables. When it is served with meat, you should use vinegar instead of lemon juice.

1 Put the wine and the same quantity of water in a fish kettle together with the onion, carrot, celery, garlic and herbs. Bring to the boil and boil for 15 minutes.

2 Cover a steamer rack with lettuce leaves.

3 Wash the fish inside and out and season with salt and pepper. Place it on the lettuce leaves and cook in the fish kettle for 10 minutes. Remove the kettle from the heat and leave the fish cool, tightly covered.

4 Make the salsa verde. In a bowl use a fork to mix together the garlic, parsley and capers. Slowly add the oil, beating the whole time to incorporate it. Add lemon juice to taste and season with salt and pepper.

5 When the fish is cold transfer it to an oval serving dish, Gently peel off the skin (it should come away easily with the scales). Pour over the oil and serve with the salsa verde.

Braised veal shanks with gremolata
Ossobuchi alla milanese

SERVES 4

4 veal shanks, about
  250 g (8 oz) each

50 g (2 oz) butter

1 tablespoon olive oil

2 shallots, finely
  chopped

flour, for coating

200 ml (7 fl oz) dry
  white wine

200 ml (7 fl oz) meat
  stock

sea salt and pepper

GREMOLATA

grated rind of
  1 unwaxed organic
  lemon

2 tablespoons chopped
  flat leaf parsley

2 garlic cloves

*There are two recipes for ossobuchi, one made without tomatoes,
which is the original recipe from Milan found below, the other
with tomatoes from Emilia-Romagna, which was created in the
19th century when tomatoes became popular in northern Italy.
Traditionally served with Risotto with saffron (see page 42).*

1 Tie the shanks across and around with cooking string as
if they were small parcels. This will help them keep their
shape while they cook.

2 Heat the butter and oil in a saucepan that is large
enough to hold the veal in a single layer. Add the shallot
and cook for about 10 minutes or until it is just beginning
to colour.

3 Meanwhile, coat the veal with flour seasoned with a
little salt. Add the meat to the onion in the pan and
brown well on both sides. Season with a little salt and
some pepper.

4 Pour over the wine and boil rapidly for 5 minutes,
turning the veal over once or twice. Add a little of the
stock, cover with a lid and cook over a low heat for about
2 hours. Carefully turn and baste the veal every 15 minutes
or so, adding a little more stock whenever the liquids dry
up. If, by the time the meat is tender, there is too much
liquid in the pan, lift out the meat, keep it warm and boil
briskly to reduce the sauce.

5 Make the gremolata. Mix together the lemon rind,
parsley and garlic and season with a little pepper.

6 Arrange the veal on a warm serving plate. Sprinkle
the gremolata over the top and serve.

Rabbit in sweet-and-sour sauce
Coniglio in dolce-forte

SERVES 4

1 rabbit, 1.25–1.5 kg (2½–3 lb), cut into pieces

30 g (1¼ oz) sultanas

1 carrot, finely chopped

2 celery sticks, finely chopped,

1 garlic clove, finely chopped

handful of fresh flat leaf parsley, chopped

1 tablespoon rosemary needles

60 g (2¼ oz) prosciutto, finely shopped

5 tablespoons olive oil

1 tablespoon flour

300 ml (½ pint) meat *or* chicken stock

125 ml (4 fl oz) good red wine vinegar

20 g (¾ oz) candied peel, cut into tiny pieces

30 g (1¼ oz) plain dark chocolate, broken into small pieces

30 g (1¼ oz) pine nuts

1½ tablespoons brown sugar, preferably muscovado

sea salt and pepper

If you are cooking wild rabbit you must allow more cooking time. The meat is cooked when it is tender. Hare can be cooked in the same way as wild rabbit.

1 Wash and dry the rabbit pieces. Soak the sultanas in a cupful of hot water to plump them up.

2 Make a *battuto* (chopped mixture) by combining the carrot, celery, garlic, parsley, rosemary and prosciutto.

4 Heat the oil in a heavy-based flameproof casserole and cook the rabbit. Add the *battuto* and turn the rabbit pieces so that they brown well all over. Sprinkle over the flour and season to taste with salt and pepper. Add the stock and cook, covered, for about 1 hour.

5 Meanwhile, make the sauce. Drain and dry the sultanas and put them in a small saucepan with the vinegar, candied peel, chocolate, pine nuts and sugar. Cook gently, stirring constantly, until the chocolate and sugar have melted.

6 Pour the sauce over the rabbit. Turn the pieces over and over and cook for a further 30 minutes or so, stirring and turning the pieces from time to time. Serve very hot with polenta (see pages 72–3).

Mackerel with peas
Lacerti con piselli

SERVES 4

4 tablespoons olive oil

4 tablespoons chopped
flat leaf parsley

1 tablespoon chopped
marjoram

1 garlic clove, finely
chopped

875 g (1¾ lb) garden
peas, shelled

4 small mackerel, each
about 200 g (7 oz)

4 tablespoons passata

sea salt and pepper

The sweetness of the peas is an ideal foil to the flavour of the fish in this recipe from Liguria.

1 Heat the oil in a heavy-based saucepan that is large enough to hold the fish. Add half the parsley, the marjoram and garlic and cook for about 1 minute. Add the peas and 4–5 tablespoons hot water. Season with salt and pepper, cover the pan and cook gently for 5–7 minutes or until the peas are cooked.

2 Meanwhile, wash and dry the fish and sprinkle some salt and pepper inside them.

3 Stir the passata into the peas and place the fish on top of the pea mixture. Cover the pan tightly and cook for 10–13 minutes or until, by lifting one side of the fish with a flat knife, you can see that the flesh is white and opaque next to the bone from which it should come easily away. (You might have to add a couple more tablespoons of hot water during the cooking, but do not add too much: there should be the minimum of liquid to concentrate the flavour.)

4 Transfer the fish to an oval serving dish and surround them with the peas. Scatter the remaining parsley all over and serve.

Calf's liver with onions
Fegato alla veneziana

SERVES 4

50 g (2 oz) unsalted butter

4 tablespoons vegetable oil

750 g (1½ lb) onions, finely sliced

700 g (1 lb 7 oz) calf's liver, finely sliced

sea salt and pepper

1 tablespoon chopped flat leaf parsley

This classic recipe from Venice is traditionally served with fried polenta (see page 73).

1 Heat the butter and oil in a frying pan that is large enough to hold the liver in a single layer. Add the onions, mix well and cook gently for 30 minutes. The onion should be very soft and just coloured. Stir occasionally during the cooking, pressing the onions against the side of the pan to release the juices.

2 When the onions are cooked lift them out of the pan with a slotted spoon and set aside. Increase the temperature and add the liver. Fry for 2 minutes on each side. Do not overcook the liver, which should be pink inside. Return the onions to the pan. Season with salt and pepper, stir thoroughly and sprinkle with the parsley. Serve immediately.

Cuttlefish stewed in wine
Seppie alla veneziana

SERVES 4
500 g (1 lb) cuttlefish
100 ml (3½ fl oz) olive oil
2 garlic cloves, crushed
2 tablespoons chopped
  flat leaf parsley
250 ml (8 fl oz) dry
  white wine
3–4 tablespoons cognac
sea salt and pepper

Cuttlefish are similar to squid but have a more pronounced flavour. They are popular all over Italy, but the best recipes are from Venice, like this one.

1 Ask your fishmonger to clean and peel the fish and to give you 3 ink sacs. When you get home, thoroughly wash the cuttlefish and cut the sacs into strips, reserving the ink, and the tentacles into pieces. Dry with kitchen paper.

2 Heat the oil in a heavy, heatproof casserole, preferably earthenware, add the garlic and parsley and fry for 1–2 minutes. Add the cuttlefish, season with salt and pepper and cook for about 5 minutes over a high heat, turning constantly.

3 Pour in the wine, let it partly evaporate and then mix in the ink from the sacs. Put the lid slightly askew on the casserole so that steam can escape and cook over a low heat for 40–45 minutes or until the cuttlefish is tender.

4 Flame the cognac in a ladle and pour it into the casserole. Mix well and continue cooking for about 5 minutes. Serve with polenta (see pages 72–3).

Beef braised in milk and vinegar

Manzo alla california

SERVES 6–8

150 g (5 oz) **unsalted butter**

4 shallots, finely chopped

2 tablespoons flour

1.5 kg (3 lb) beef, top rump or chuck steak, rolled and tied

1 celery stick, chopped

3 medium carrots, chopped

75 ml (3 fl oz) red wine vinegar

450 ml (¾ pint) full-fat milk

4 tablespoons double cream

sea salt and pepper

This California has nothing to do with the American California. It is a district in the outskirts of Milan, now part of the city.

1 Heat the butter in a heavy, flameproof casserole and cook the shallots for 2–3 minutes until soft.

2 Meanwhile, spread the flour on a board, season it with a pinch of salt and lightly coat the beef with it. Add the meat to the casserole and brown well on all sides and the ends.

3 Add the celery and carrots and fry gently for 5 minutes, stirring frequently. Pour over the vinegar and boil rapidly to reduce. Add the milk, bring to the boil, cover the pan with a piece of foil and then with the lid to seal it well. Simmer for about 3 hours, until the meat is tender when pricked with a fork. Turn the meat over 2–3 times during the cooking and add a few tablespoons of water if the sauce becomes too dry.

4 Transfer the meat to a plate. Skim off and discard excess fat from the sauce, then purée it in a liquidizer or a food processor or with a stick blender. Return the sauce to the casserole and boil rapidly for 3–4 minutes to reduce. Add the cream, taste and adjust the seasonings.

5 Cut the meat into slices about 1 cm (½ inch) thick and arrange them, slightly overlapping, on a warm serving dish. Cover with some sauce and pour the remaining sauce into a sauce boat. Serve with mashed potatoes or polenta (see pages 72–3).

Veal in tuna sauce
Vitello tonnato

1 kg (2 lb) fillet of veal

75 ml (3 fl oz) dry white
wine

75 ml (3 fl oz) wine
vinegar

1 small carrot

½ celery stick

1 onion stuck with
1 clove

sprig of flat leaf parsley

several whole black
peppercorns

200 g (7 oz) can tuna,
drained and chopped

4 anchovy fillets,
chopped

1 tablespoon capers

sea salt and pepper

black olives, to garnish

MAYONNAISE

2 egg yolks, beaten

3 teaspoons organic
lemon juice

ground black pepper

250–300 ml (8–10 fl oz)
olive oil

*There are two versions of this well-known dish, one from Milan
without mayonnaise and the other from Piedmont with mayonnaise.
This is the Piedmontese version.*

1 Put the veal, wine, vinegar, carrot, celery, onion, parsley,
salt and a few peppercorns in a saucepan together with
150 ml (¼ pint) of water and bring to the boil. Simmer
gently for about 1 hour or until the meat is tender.

2 Meanwhile, make the mayonnaise by adding the egg
yolks, lemon juice and pepper to a bowl and beating with a
balloon whisk to combine. Whisking continuously, gradually
pour in the oil in a thin, steady stream until the sauce starts
to thicken. Continue adding the oil until the consistency is
thick and glossy. Don't add the oil too quickly, otherwise the
mixture might start to separate. Whenever the mayonnaise
becomes too thick, beat in a little lemon juice to thin it. Do
not add salt: the anchovies and the cooking liquid should
make the sauce sufficiently salty.

3 Lift the meat out of the pan and set aside to cool. Drain
the vegetables, reserving the cooking liquid, and put the
vegetables in a blender or food processor, add the tuna and
anchovies and a few tablespoons of the cooking liquid.
Process to make a purée and transfer to a bowl.

4 Mix the mayonnaise into the tuna and vegetable
mixture and add the capers and pepper. Stir in enough
cooking liquid to give the sauce the consistency of double
cream. Stir well, taste and add salt if necessary.

5 When the meat is cold cut it into slices 1 cm (½ inch)
thick and arrange them, slightly overlapping, on a serving
dish. Cover with the tuna mayonnaise, scatter over the
olives and serve.

Chicken with truffle cream sauce
Pollo alla panna con i tartufi

SERVES 4

4 chicken legs, halved

25 g (1 oz) unsalted butter

150 ml (¼ pint) double cream

2 teaspoons truffle paste

2 tablespoons chopped flat leaf parsley

sea salt and pepper

Some of the traditional recipes from Lombardy contain cream, which is very seldom used in the other regions of Italy. This simple recipe is absolutely delicious with a truffle grated over the top just before serving, but if you do not have the real thing, use truffle paste instead.

1 Wash and dry the chicken pieces thoroughly. Heat the butter in a large, flameproof casserole and, when the foam begins to subside, add the chicken pieces. Brown them quickly until they are a light golden colour all over. Season the chicken with salt and pepper and pour over the cream.

2 Cover the casserole, bring to the boil and then put the casserole in a preheated oven, 180°C (350°F), Gas Mark 4, and cook for about 1 hour. Turn the chicken pieces 2–3 times during the cooking.

3 Put the truffle paste in a bowl and pour over it about 200 ml (7 fl oz) of the chicken and cream sauce from the casserole. Beat thoroughly, then pour the mixture back into the casserole. Mix again, check the seasoning, sprinkle with the chopped parsley and serve immediately.

Red mullet in a piquant tomato sauce
Triglie alla livornese

SERVES 4

4 fresh red mullet, each about 225 g (7½ oz)

4 tablespoons olive oil

½ garlic clove, finely chopped

3 tablespoons chopped flat leaf parsley

1 small celery stalk, preferably with its leaves, finely chopped

1 dried chilli, very finely chopped

225 g (7½ oz) can chopped tomatoes

sea salt and pepper

The liver of the fish should be left in the cavity, being considered a delicacy. Red mullet is one of the few white fish tasty enough to be cooked in a lively sauce, such as this.

1 Whether or not you have cleaned them, wash and dry the fish. Sprinkle them with salt and pepper inside and out.

2 Heat 2 tablespoons of the oil in a small frying pan, add the garlic, half the parsley, the celery and chilli and cook for about 2 minutes. Add the tomatoes and cook for about 10 minutes at a lively simmer to concentrate the flavours.

3 Meanwhile, heat the remaining oil in a frying pan that is large enough to hold the fish in a single layer. When the oil is very hot, slide in the fish and cook for 3 minutes. Turn them over very gently and cook for a further 2 minutes.

4 Spoon the tomato sauce over the fish and cook for a further 10 minutes. Season to taste with salt and pepper. Sprinkle over the remaining parsley and serve immediately.

Milanese veal escalopes
Cotolette alla milanese

SERVES 4

500 g (1 lb) veal escalopes

1 egg, lightly beaten

150 g (5 oz) dried white breadcrumbs

100 g (3½ oz) unsalted butter

1 tablespoon olive oil

sea salt

unwaxed organic lemon wedges, to serve

One of the best known dishes of Milanese cuisine, this recipe can also be made with veal chops.

1 If the escalopes are large, cut them in half. Beat the veal gently with a meat mallet or rolling pin until it is quite thin and season with salt.

2 Put the egg in a shallow bowl and put the breadcrumbs in another bowl. Dip each escalope in the beaten egg, letting any excess egg drip back into the bowl, then coat them with breadcrumbs. Press the crumbs firmly into the surface of the escalope with the palm of your hands.

3 Heat the butter and oil in a large frying pan and when the foam begins to subside add the escalopes in a single layer. Fry on both sides until golden. If thin, the escalopes need only a few minutes cooking – no more than 2 minutes on each side. When they are cooked transfer them to on a warm dish and keep warm. Serve with lemon wedges.

Tuna steaks in sweet-and-sour sauce

Trance di tonno in agrodolce

SERVES 4

4 tuna steaks, each about 200 g (7 oz)

5 tablespoons wine vinegar, preferably red

3 tablespoons olive oil

2 Spanish onions, cut into rings

2 tablespoons tomato purée, diluted in 225 ml (7½ fl oz) warm water

2 teaspoons caster sugar

sea salt and pepper

In this recipe from southern Italy, the sweet-and-sour sauce counteracts the richness of the fish in a most appetizing way. Tuna fish steaks should be deep pink, not deep red and not too thickly cut: 2–2.5 cm (¾–1 inch) thick is ideal.

1 Cover the fish with cold water, add 1 tablespoon salt and half the vinegar. Leave for 2 hours.

2 Heat the oil in a pan that is large enough to accommodate the fish in a single layer. Add the onions and fry, stirring frequently, until soft and deep golden.

3 Lift the fish out of the marinade and dry thoroughly with kitchen paper. Add to the onions in the pan and cook for 5 minutes, turning once. Add the diluted tomato purée, the remaining vinegar and the sugar. Mix gently, cover the pan and cook over low heat for 10–15 minutes or until the fish is done. (This will depend on the thickness of the steaks.) Turn the steaks once during the cooking. Taste and adjust the seasoning, adding some ground black pepper if liked. Serve the tuna hot or warm or at room temperature.

Chicken with tomato sauce
Pollo in potacchio

SERVES 4

4 large fresh chicken joints, halved

½ unwaxed organic lemon

2 tablespoons olive oil

50 g (2 oz) unsalted butter

2 garlic cloves, finely chopped

1 onion, roughly chopped

150 ml (¼ pint) dry white wine

sea salt and pepper

POTACCHIO

3 tablespoons olive oil

2 shallots *or* 1 small onion, finely chopped

3 sprigs of rosemary, each about 12 cm (5 inches) long, finely chopped

500 g tomatoes, skinned and coarsely chopped *or* 400 g (13 oz) can plum tomatoes, drained and roughly chopped

grated rind of 1 unwaxed organic lemon

1–2 dried chillies (to taste), deseeded and finely chopped

sea salt

The sauce, known as potacchio, *is popular in Le Marche, where it is served with rabbit, chicken or fish.*

1 Wash and dry the chicken pieces and rub each with lemon.

2 Heat the oil and butter in a large, heatproof casserole. Add the garlic, onion and chicken pieces and fry for about 5 minutes on each side until the chicken is pale golden. Season to taste with salt and pepper. Remove the chicken from the casserole and keep warm.

3 Pour off most of the fat left in the casserole. Add the wine and boil rapidly for 1 minute. Add 2 tablespoons warm water and bring to the boil, scraping up the sediment left in the bottom of the casserole with a spoon. Season to taste with salt and pepper. Return the chicken to the casserole, cover and cook in a preheated oven, 180°C (350°F), Gas Mark 4, for 20 minutes.

4 Meanwhile, prepare the sauce. Heat the oil in a saucepan, add the shallots or onion and the rosemary and fry gently for 5 minutes. Add the tomatoes, lemon rind and chilli and season to taste with salt. Cook, uncovered, over a low heat for 15 minutes. Adjust the seasonings. (By the time the sauce is ready, the chicken should have been removed from the oven.)

5 Pour the sauce over the chicken, mixing it with the sediment in the casserole, and return the casserole, covered, to the oven for a further 15 minutes. Check that the chicken is cooked by piercing a drumstick with the point of a sharp knife or a skewer. The juices should run clear. Serve piping hot with new or mashed potatoes.

Lamb marinated in wine
Agnello al capretto

SERVES 4-5

butt end of a leg of
lamb, about 1.5 kg
(3 lb)

2 tablespoons olive oil

sea salt

MARINADE
1 onion, chopped

4 garlic cloves, crushed

2 sprigs of flat leaf
parsley

2 bay leaves

1 sprig of rosemary

1 sprig of sage

2 tablespoons olive oil

2 cloves

10 juniper berries,
slightly crushed

10 peppercorns, slightly
crushed

200 ml (7 fl oz) red wine

100 ml (3½ fl oz) red
wine vinegar

The Italian name of this dish, agnello al capretto, *means 'kid-style lamb'. This is because the marinating of the lamb in wine, vinegar, herbs and spices gives the meat a strong, slightly gamey flavour.*

1 Make the marinade. Put the onion, garlic, parsley, bay leaf, rosemary, sage and oil in a saucepan and fry gently for 5 minutes. Add the cloves, juniper berries, peppercorns, wine and vinegar and simmer for 10 minutes over a gentle heat. Allow the marinade to cool and then pour it over the lamb. Leave to marinate for at least 24 hours, turning the meat over and basting it as often as you remember.

2 Remove the meat and strain the marinade, discarding the herbs and spices. Dry the lamb thoroughly with kitchen paper.

3 Heat the oil in a large frying pan, add the meat and brown well on all sides to seal.

4 Transfer the lamb to a heatproof casserole and pour over the strained marinade. Bring slowly to the boil, season with salt and put the casserole, covered, in a preheated oven, 200°C (400°F), Gas Mark 6, and cook until the lamb is tender, basting regularly. If you like lamb just pink, 1½ hours will be enough; otherwise cook for an extra 15–20 minutes. Transfer the meat to a heated dish and keep warm.

5 Skim off as much fat as you can from the surface of the cooking liquid. Taste and check the seasoning. If it is bland, boil sharply to reduce. Pour the cooking liquid into a sauceboat and serve with the meat carved into thick slices.

Baked fresh sardines
Tortino di sardine

SERVES 4

750 g (1½ lb) sardines
or sprats

5 level tablespoons
fresh breadcrumbs

4 tablespoons olive oil,
plus extra for greasing

2 tablespoons wine
vinegar

1 tablespoon capers

1 garlic clove, crushed

1 tablespoon chopped
marjoram

sea salt and pepper

Sprats can also be used in this recipe because they are often fresher than sardines. You can also use frozen sardines, although they are less tasty than the fresh fish.

1 Remove the heads and tails from the fish, open them and gently ease out and discard the backbones. Wash the fish under cold running water and pat them dry with kitchen paper.

2 Put all the other ingredients in a bowl and mix well together.

3 Grease a shallow, 20 cm (8 inch) round ovenproof dish with oil and cover the base with a layer of the fish, arranged like the petals of a flower. Spread half the sauce evenly over it. Cover with another layer of fish and then the remaining sauce.

4 Bake in a preheated oven, 200°C (400°F), Gas Mark 6, for 15 minutes. Serve hot or cold, but neither straight from the oven not straight from the refrigerator.

Basic frittata

SERVES 4

6 eggs

75 g (3 oz) grated Parmesan cheese

40 g (1½ oz) unsalted butter

sea salt and pepper

In Italy, frittata is traditionally eaten by itself but, if you like, you can hand around a bowl of green salad as an accompaniment. Frittata can be eaten hot, warm or at room temperature.

1 In a large bowl lightly beat the eggs together. Add the Parmesan and season to taste with salt and pepper.

2 Melt the butter in a 25 cm (10 inch) frying pan with a heatproof handle and, when the foam begins to subside, add the egg and cheese mixture. Turn down the heat and cook for 5–10 minutes until the mixture is firm and only the top is runny.

3 Put the frying pan under a preheated hot grill and cook until the top is set but not hard. Loosen the frittata with a palette knife and transfer to a round serving dish.

Frittata with onions
Frittata di cipolle

SERVES 4

2 tablespoons olive oil

3 large onions, finely sliced

5 eggs, beaten

40 g (1½ oz) unsalted butter

sea salt and pepper

Frittatas are an excellent way to use up leftovers and can also be made with courgettes, peppers, mushrooms, spinach and most other vegetables (see page 110). A particularly delicious frittata can be made with leftover spaghetti.

1 Heat the oil in a 25 cm (10 inch) frying pan with a heatproof handle, add the onions and cook over a low heat until soft and golden.

2 Use a fish slice or slotted spoon to transfer the onion to a bowl. Add the beaten eggs and seasoning and mix together thoroughly.

3 Melt the butter in the frying pan and cook the frittata as described on page 108.

Frittata with courgettes
Frittata di zucchine

SERVES 4

350 g (11½ oz)
  courgettes

2 tablespoons olive oil

2 garlic cloves, sliced

2 tablespoons chopped
  flat leaf parsley

6 eggs, lightly beaten

1 tablespoon dried
  oregano

6 tablespoons grated
  Parmesan cheese

30 g (1¼ oz) unsalted
  butter

sea salt and pepper

No matter what vegetable you prefer to use in a frittata – fennel, mushrooms, artichokes or onion – the method for making it is the same as in this recipe.

1 Wash and dry the courgettes and then cut them into matchsticks.

2 Heat the oil in a medium-sized frying pan, add the garlic and parsley and cook for 1–2 minutes. Add the courgettes and cook, stirring frequently, for about 10 minutes or until brown.

3 Meanwhile, put the eggs in a bowl, season to taste with salt and pepper and add the oregano and Parmesan.

4 When the courgettes are cooked, lift them out of the pan with a slotted spoon and add them to the eggs. Cook the frittata as described on page 108.

Contorni

Potatoes with parsley and garlic
Patate trifolate

SERVES 4−6

1 kg (2 lb) waxy
potatoes

2 tablespoons olive oil

30 g (1¼ oz) unsalted
butter

3 tablespoons chopped
flat leaf parsley

2 garlic cloves, chopped

sea salt and pepper

The word trifolate *means to cook gently in oil with garlic and parsley. It is a method often used with potatoes, as here, and mushrooms (see page 118) but also with aubergines and courgettes.*

1 Peel the potatoes, cut them into 15 mm (¾ inch) cubes and dry them thoroughly with kitchen paper.

2 Heat the oil and butter in a large, heavy-based frying pan or sautée pan, add the parsley and garlic and cook for 1 minute. Add the potatoes and cook over a moderate heat for 6–7 minutes, turning the potatoes frequently.

3 Pour 100 ml (3½ fl oz) boiling water into the pan and season to taste with salt and pepper. Turn down the heat to low, cover and continue cooking until the potatoes are soft. Stir occasionally with a fork (not a spoon), which is less likely to break the potatoes cubes. If necessary, top up with a little more boiling water.

Spinach sautéed in oil and lemon
Spinaci all'agro

SERVES 4

1 kg (2 lb) bunch spinach

6 tablespoons olive oil

3 garlic cloves, lightly crushed

juice of 1 unwaxed organic lemon (to taste)

sea salt and pepper

In Italy bunch spinach – spinach that is not separated into leaves – is used for this simple dish.

1 To clean a bunch of spinach, scrape the roots clean and then cut each bunch in half and put in a sink of cold water. Wash in 3 or 4 changes of water, if necessary, until clean.

2 Put the spinach and 1 teaspoon salt in a saucepan with the water which clings to the spinach leaves after washing. Cover the pan and cook over high heat until the spinach is tender, turning it over a few times while it cooks. Drain but do not overdrain.

3 Heat the oil in a frying pan and add the garlic. When the oil is hot add the spinach and fry over a gentle heat for about 8 minutes, turning frequently. Remove and discard the garlic (if liked) and add lemon juice and pepper. Mix well and serve.

Stewed carrots
Carote stufate

SERVES 4

30 g (1¼ oz) unsalted
  butter

1 tablespoon olive oil

½ onion, finely chopped

500 g (1 lb) carrots

1 teaspoon caster sugar

1 teaspoon flour

100 ml (3½ fl oz)
  vegetable stock

sea salt and pepper

This is one of the most common ways of cooking carrots and the result is delicious.

1 Heat the the butter and oil in a saucepan, add the onion and cook for about 5 minutes over a gentle heat to soften the onion; do not let the onion become brown.

2 Cut the carrots into 5 cm (2 inch) pieces and then cut each piece into matchsticks. Add the carrots to the onion and cook for 5 minutes. Mix in the sugar and flour and cook, stirring, for 1 minute. Season to taste with salt and pepper and pour in the stock. Bring to the boil, cover the pan and cook over a gentle heat for 15–20 minutes or until the carrots are tender. Stir occasionally. If there is too much liquid when the carrots are tender, uncover the pan and cook over high heat for 1 or 2 minutes. On the other hand, if the carrots are catching before they are properly cooked, add 2 or 3 tablespoons of boiling water. Check the seasoning and serve.

Mushrooms with parsley and garlic
Funghi trifolati

SERVES 4

500 g (1 lb) porcini *or* cultivated mushrooms *or* a mixture of the two

5 tablespoons olive oil

2 garlic cloves, finely chopped

3 tablespoons chopped flat leaf parsley

sea salt and pepper

This method of cooking is used mostly with porcini mushrooms but is also suitable for cultivated mushrooms, or a mixture of the two.

1 Clean the mushrooms with kitchen paper and slice them.

2 Heat the oil in a frying pan, add the garlic and half the parsley and cook for about 1 minute. Add the mushrooms and cook over high heat for about 3 minutes or until they have absorbed all the oil.

3 Turn the heat down, season to taste with salt and pepper and continue cooking. When the juice has come out of the mushrooms, turn the heat up again and cook briskly for about 5 minutes, stirring very frequently, until there is not much liquid in the pan.

4 Sprinkle over the remaining parsley, mix well and serve.

Broccoli sautéed in oil and garlic

Broccoli strascinati

SERVES 4
750 g (1½ lb) broccoli
4 tablespoons olive oil
2 garlic cloves, sliced
1 dried chilli, deseeded
   and quartered
sea salt

For this recipe only the florets of the broccoli are required. Keep the stems and leaves for another meal. Cauliflower can be prepared in the same way.

1 Separate the florets from the stem and leaves, and, if they are large, cut the florets in half. Wash thoroughly.

2 Heat the oil in a frying pan that is large enough to hold the broccoli in a single layer and add the garlic and the chilli. When the garlic begins to colour add the broccoli. Season with salt and cook for 1–2 minutes.

3 Turn the heat down and cover the pan. Cook for 12–15 minutes until the broccoli is tender. Turn them over from time to time and, if they appear too dry, add a few tablespoons of boiling water. When they are cooked, remove and discard the chilli and check the seasoning. Serve hot or warm or at room temperature.

Peppers stewed with tomatoes
Peperonata

SERVES 4

1 kg (2 lb) yellow and
red peppers

100 ml (3½ fl oz) olive oil

4 medium onions,
chopped

500 g (1 lb) ripe
tomatoes, peeled

2 tablespoons balsamic
vinegar

sea salt and pepper

In the traditional recipe for peperonata *wine vinegar is used.
I prefer to use balsamic vinegar, which is slightly sweeter.*

1 Wash and dry the peppers and cut them in half. Remove the seeds and white ribs and cut them in 2 cm (¾ inch) strips.

2 Heat the oil in a saucepan, add the onion and a pinch or two of salt and cook until the onion is translucent. Mix in the peppers.

3 Cut the tomatoes into segments and add them to the pan. Mix well and cook over moderate heat for about 5 minutes.

4 Turn down the heat, add 2 tablespoons water and continue cooking for about 20 minutes or until the peppers are just tender.

5 Add the vinegar, season with pepper and cook for 5 minutes. Taste and adjust the seasoning. Serve warm or at room temperature.

French beans with tomatoes

Fagiolini alla fiorentina

SERVES 4
500 g (1 lb) French
  beans, tails trimmed

4 tablespoons olive oil

1 shallot, finely sliced

1 teaspoons fennel
  seeds

350 g (11 ½ oz) ripe
  tomatoes, peeled,
  deseeded and
  roughly chopped

sea salt and pepper

In Tuscany several dishes are flavoured with fennel, which grows wild everywhere. In this recipe they partner French beans.

1 Blanch the beans for 3 minutes in plenty of boiling salted water. Drain.

2 Heat the oil in a frying pan, add the shallot and cook for about 5 minutes until soft and golden. Stir frequently, pressing the shallot against the side of the frying pan to release the juices.

3 Add the fennel seeds and beans, season to taste with salt and pepper and cook for 5 minutes. Add the tomatoes and continue cooking for about 20 minutes, stirring occasionally. Taste and adjust the seasoning.

Fried cauliflower
Cavolfiore fritto

SERVES 4
1 cauliflower
oil, for frying
flour
1 egg, lightly beaten
sea salt

Many vegetables are deep-fried in this way, and then served on their own or as an accompaniment to grilled or fried meat or fish.

1 Prepare the cauliflower by detaching the florets from the central stalk. (Keep the stalk for a vegetable soup.) Make sure that all the florets are small and more or less the same size, then wash and drain them. Dry them on kitchen paper. Blanch them for 3–4 minutes in boiling salted water.

2 Add sufficient oil to a wok or large frying pan to come 6–7 cm (2½–3 inches) up the sides. Heat it until very hot but not smoking.

3 Meanwhile, spoon 2–3 tablespoons flour into a plastic bag. Add the florets, shake the bag and then turn it upside down on a board. Pick out the florets one by one, shake lightly and coat them in the egg. Slide them into the hot oil and cook for about 5 minutes. Do not put too many in the wok at once or they will not fry well. Lift them out with a slotted spoon and put them on 2–3 pieces of kitchen paper to drain. Sprinkle with salt and keep warm until you are ready to serve.

Peas with prosciutto
Piselli al prosciutto

SERVES 4

3 tablespoons olive oil

1 small sweet onion,
finely chopped

1 kg (2 lb) fresh peas,
unshelled weight, *or*
300 g (10 oz) frozen
petits pois, thawed

50 g (2 oz) prosciutto,
cut into short strips

sea salt and pepper

This is the traditional way to cook peas in Tuscany. The prosciutto is a tasty foil to the sweetness of the peas, thus giving the dish a more interesting and complex flavour.

1 Heat the oil in a saucepan, add the oil and fry for about 5 minutes or until translucent. Season with a pinch of salt. Add the peas and, if you are using fresh peas, a couple of tablespoons of hot water.

2 Turn down the heat to low, cover the pan and cook for 5 minutes (for fresh peas) or 3 minutes (for frozen peas).

3 When the peas are cooked add the prosciutto, mix well and cook for a further minute. Season with pepper and, if necessary, salt but be careful with it, because some prosciutto can be quite salty.

Stewed artichokes and broad beans
Carciofi e fave stufati

SERVES 4

4–5 small globe
artichokes

4 tablespoons organic
lemon juice

3 tablespoons olive oil

1 garlic clove, chopped

2 sprigs of thyme

200 ml (7 fl oz) vegetable
stock

300 g (10 oz) young
broad beans (shelled
weight)

2 tablespoons chopped
flat leaf parsley

1 tablespoon chopped
mint

sea salt and pepper

You will need small artichokes for this dish from Rome, and you must discard all the tough, outer leaves so that you are able to eat the whole pieces of artichokes. Peas can be used instead of broad beans.

1 Cut off the stems of the artichokes. Peel off and discard the outer skin of the stems and cut the stems into chunks. Trim away the outer leaves of the artichokes until you get to the paler green leaves. Slice off about 2 cm (¾ inch) from the top. Cut each artichoke in quarters, remove the choke and the soft purplish leaves and cut each quarter in half. Rub each cut part and each chunk of stem with lemon juice and put the pieces in acidulated water (water with the juice of half a lemon squeezed into it).

2 Drain the artichokes and the stems. Put the artichokes cut side up in an earthenware casserole into which they fit snugly. Tuck the stems between them and add the oil, garlic, thyme, stock and salt and pepper and cook in a preheated oven, 180°C (350°F), Gas Mark 4, for about 20 minutes. Add the beans and cook for a further 7–9 minutes. (The cooking time will depend on the age and quality of the vegetables.) Test with a fork or the point of a small knife inserted into the thickest bit of stem or simply pull off an outside leaf and taste.

3 When the vegetables are cooked, sprinkle over the parsley and mint and serve.

Fennel with butter and Parmesan
Finocchi alla milanese

SERVES 4

4 fennel bulbs

50 g (2 oz) unsalted
butter

1 tablespoon olive oil

4 tablespoons grated
Parmesan cheese

sea salt

The original cooking fat of Lombardy is butter, not olive oil. This is because of the abundance of cows due to the richness of the pasture of the Lombard plain and the absence of olive trees due to the cold winters. Most vegetables used to be finished as in this recipe, with butter and cheese.

1 Remove any bruised and brown parts of the fennel and cut off and discard the tops. Cut the bulbs into quarters, wash them and then cut them into segments.

2 Heat the butter and oil in a saucepan and add the fennel segments. Cook, turning them over, for 5 minutes. Pour in enough hot water to cover the bottom of the pan. Season with a little salt. Cover the pan with a lid and continue cooking for a further 10 minutes, turning the fennel from time to time.

3 Uncover the pan and continue to cook until the fennel is tender and the liquid has been absorbed. Add the Parmesan, mix thoroughly and serve.

Dolci

Strawberries with balsamic vinegar
Fragole all'aceto balsemico

SERVES 4

750 g (1½ lb) strawberries

2–3 tablespoons caster sugar

3 tablespoons balsamic vinegar

The sweet acidity of the balsamic vinegar brings out the flavour of the strawberries. This is the traditional way of serving strawberries in Emilia-Romagna where the balsamic vinegar is produced.

1 Wash and hull the strawberries. Gently dry them with kitchen paper and then halve or quarter the larger fruits. The small pieces soak up more juice and become more flavoursome.

2 About 2 hours before serving sprinkle the strawberries with the sugar and toss gently but thoroughly.

3 About 30 minutes before serving pour the vinegar over the strawberries and toss again. Immediately before serving, spoon into glass cups or flutes.

Tiramisu

SERVES 6

2 tablespoons caster sugar

4 tablespoons brandy

200 ml (7 fl oz) espresso coffee

60 g (2¼ oz) plain dark chocolate, chopped

2 eggs

50 g (2 oz) icing sugar, sieved

400 g (13 oz) mascarpone cheese

200 g (7 oz) savoiardi biscuits

2 teaspoons cocoa powder

This, possibly the best-known Italian pudding, is a relatively modern creation, dating from after the Second World War. Here is the classic recipe, which came from Treviso in Veneto.

1 Put the caster sugar in a small saucepan, add the brandy, coffee and chocolate and heat gently until the sugar and chocolate have dissolved. Leave to cool.

2 Beat the eggs and icing sugar until light and frothy, then beat in the mascarpone.

3 Dip the biscuits into the coffee mixture and lay them close together over the bottom of a shallow rectangular dish, filling any gaps between them. Spread over the mascarpone cream. Cover the dish with clingfilm and put it in the refrigerator to chill overnight.

4 Before serving put the cocoa powder in a small sieve and sprinkle it over the top in a thin, even layer.

Pistachio ice cream

Gelato di pistacchio

SERVES 4 – 6
500 ml (17 fl oz) full-fat milk
1 vanilla pod
4 egg yolks
125 g (4 oz) caster sugar
2 pinches of ground cinnamon
200 g (7 oz) fresh pistachios, coarsely chopped

The best pistachios come from Bronte, a town at the foot of Mount Etna in Sicily. This is the recipe for the ice cream made there.

1 Put the milk in a saucepan, add the vanilla pod and bring to simmering point. Leave to infuse for at least 20 minutes, then remove the vanilla pod. (You can wash and dry it and keep it for another time.)

2 Beat the egg yolks with the sugar until light and forming ribbons. Slowly add the milk, beating the whole time. Transfer the custard to a heavy-based saucepan and heat slowly, beating constantly. The custard will thicken slowly. When it is very hot but before it starts boiling, remove the pan from the heat or the custard will curdle. Add the cinnamon and put the pan immediately in a bowl of cold water so that the custard cools quickly. Stir frequently while it cools.

3 When the custard is cold mix in the pistachio nuts and transfer the custard mixture to an ice cream machine to finish. Alternatively, make the ice cream by hand. Transfer the custard mixture to a freezer container and freeze until a 3 cm (1¼ inch) band of custard has frozen around th edges. Scrape the mixture into the soft centre with a balloon whisk or hand-held electric whisk until no lumps remain. Refreeze until a thicker band of custard has frozen around the edges. Whisk again and freeze until firm. For a creamier flavour, repeat the whisking and freezing process once or twice.

Cake and custard pudding

Zuppa Inglese

SERVES 6

150 ml (¼ pint) double cream

350 g (11½ oz) good-quality Madeira cake, cut into 5 mm (¼ inch) slices

4 tablespoons rum

4 tablespoons cherry brandy

almonds, to decorate

CUSTARD

500 ml (17 fl oz) full-fat milk

2 strips of unwaxed organic lemon rind

3 egg yolks

75 g (3 oz) caster sugar

50 g (2 oz) plain flour

The odd name of this pudding, suppa inglese *(English soup), probably derives from the fact that it is the Italian version of* trifle, *which the English brought to Tuscany in the 19th century. Traditionally, the liqueurs used are rum and alchermes, a flowery liqueur not easily found outside Italy. Cherry brandy is a good substitute.*

1 Make the custard. Put the milk in a saucepan with the lemon rind, bring to the boil and set aside.

2 Beat the egg yolks with the sugar until pale and frothy. Beat the flour into the mixture, then slowly pour in the hot milk.

3 Transfer the custard to a heavy-based saucepan and cook over a very low heat, stirring continuously, until the custard becomes thick and an occasional bubble breaks through the surface. Simmer gently for a couple of minutes longer. Place the base of the saucepan in a bowl of iced water to cool the custard quickly. Stir frequently.

4 Whip the cream until soft peaks form. When the custard is cold, fold in the cream.

5 Line the bottom of a 2-litre (3½-pint) glass bowl with slices of cake, filling any gaps with pieces of cake. Sprinkle over some rum and spread a couple of spoonfuls of custard over the cake.

6 Cover with another layer of cake, moisten it with cherry brandy and then spread over some custard. Repeat these layers, ending with a layer of custard.

7 Cover the bowl with clingfilm, put it in the refrigerator and chill for at least 8 hours to allow the flavours to combine. Sprinkle with almonds before serving.

Chocolate and hazelnut cake

Torta di cioccolato

SERVES 8–10

250 g (8 oz) plain dark
chocolate, chopped

500 g (1 lb) hazelnuts

5 tablespoons brandy

1 teaspoons ground
cinnamon

2 tablespoons full-fat
milk

225 g (7½ oz) caster
sugar

5 eggs, separated

1½ tablespoons grated
unwaxed organic
orange rind

unsalted butter, for
greasing

dried breadcrumbs, for
the tin

This is a simpler version of the celebrated torta gianduja *from
Turin. It is an ideal cake for any occasion and can even be eaten
as a pudding, served with some pouring cream.*

1 Put the chocolate in a food processor, add the hazelnuts
and process until the mixture has a grainy consistency but
is not finely ground. Transfer the mixture to a bowl and
stir in the brandy, cinnamon, milk and sugar. Mix
together thoroughly.

2 Lightly beat the egg yolks and mix them into the
chocolate mixture together with the orange rind.

3 Whisk the egg whites until they are stiff but not too
dry. Fold them into the chocolate mixture with a large
metal spoon, incorporating as much air as possible into
the mixture.

4 Generously butter a 23 cm (8 inch) springform cake tin.
Sprinkle with the breadcrumbs, then turn the tin upside
down and tap off any excess breadcrumbs.

5 Spoon the cake mixture into the tin and cook in a
preheated oven, 200°C (400°F), Gas Mark 6, for 45 minutes.
The cake is ready when a cocktail stick inserted into the
centre comes out dry. Turn out the cake on to a metal rack,
remove the base of the cake tin and leave to cool.

Peaches stuffed with amaretti
Pesche ripiene alla piemontese

SERVES 6

6 freestone peaches

4 tablespoons caster sugar

100 ml (3½ fl oz) Moscato wine *or* other sweet white wine

30 g (1¼ oz) unsalted butter

3 tablespoons Marsala

125 g (4 oz) amaretti

3–4 drops pure almond extract

1 egg, separated

2 tablespoons rum

2 pinches of ground cinnamon

Choose peaches that are ripe but firm and make sure that they are freestone or you might find difficult to remove the stone.

1 Wash and dry the peaches. Cut them in half, twist each half in opposite directions and remove the stones.

2 Put 2 tablespoons of the sugar and the wine in a small saucepan and bring gently to the boil. When the sugar has dissolved, pour the mixture into a shallow, ovenproof dish that is large enough to hold all the peaches.

3 Use a sharp teaspoon to scoop some of the pulp from each half, leaving about 1 cm (½ inch) of flesh all around. Set the pulp aside and arrange the peach halves, cut side up, in the prepared dish.

4 Put a tiny knob of butter in each peach half and cook in a preheated oven, 160°C (325°F), Gas Mark 3, for 10 minutes. Remove the dish from the oven and increase the temperature to 190°C (375°F), Gas Mark 5.

5 Heat the remaining butter and sugar in a small frying pan. Add the peach pulp and cook for a couple of minutes. Pour in the Marsala and cook gently for 5 minutes.

6 Put the peach pulp with all the juices in a food processor or blender, add the amaretti and the almond extract and process for a few seconds. Spoon the mixture into a bowl and mix in the egg yolk, rum and cinnamon. Beat the egg white until stiff and fold gently into the mixture.

7 Fill each peach half with the mixture. Return the dish to the oven and cook for about 20 minutes or until the top is set. Serve hot or warm.

Panna cotta

SERVES 4
150 ml (¼ pint) full-fat milk

450 ml (¾ pint) double cream

vanilla pod

100 g (3½ oz) caster sugar

4 tablespoons white rum

15 g (½ oz) gelatine leaves

Traditionally, panna cotta, a Piedmontese pudding, is served by itself without any fruit or other flavouring. Hazelnut Biscuits, Brutti ma buoni *(see page 150), are a perfect accompaniment.*

1 Put the milk and cream in a saucepan and heat gently. Cut the vanilla pod in half lengthways and scrape out the seeds. Add the seeds and the pod to the saucepan. Add the sugar and rum and bring slowly to a simmer. Simmer for 1 minute, stirring constantly, and then set aside to infuse for 1 hour. Strain into a clean bowl. (Wash and dry the vanilla pod and keep it for future use.)

2 Put the gelatine leaves in a flat dish and cover them with water. When the leaves are soft (after about 10 minutes) take them from the dish and squeeze out all the water. Put the gelatine in 4 tablespoons boiling water and, when it has completely dissolved, pour the liquid into the cream and milk mixture. Stir well.

3 Spoon the cream mixture into 4 ramekins, cover with clingfilm and chill for at least 2 hours.

4 Run a palette knife around the sides of the ramekins and turn them upside down on individual serving plates. Leave for 5 minutes and then give the ramekins a sharp shake and lift them off.

Zabaglione

SERVES 4

4 egg yolks

60 g (2¼ oz) caster sugar

4 tablespoons dry Marsala

4 tablespoons dry white wine

300 ml (½ pint) whipped cream (optional)

In Milan a pinch or two of ground cinnamon is sprinkled on the top of this dish before serving. In Sardinia Vernaccia, the local sweet wine is used and a handful of pistachio nuts are often added at the end.

1 Put the egg yolks and sugar in a heatproof bowl and use an electric whisk to beat until the mixture is pale and creamy.

2 Put some water in a large saucepan and bring it to the brink of a simmer. Set the bowl with the egg yolks over it.

3 Slowly add the Marsala and wine to the egg and sugar mixture, beating constantly. The mixture will form a light foam.

4 Spoon the pudding into glasses. If you want to serve the zabaglione cold, let it cool, stirring it frequently, and then gently fold in 300 ml (½ pint) whipped cream. Spoon into glasses and chill.

Ricotta cake
Torta di ricotta

SERVES 6

2 tablespoons orange water

30 sultanas

150 g (5 oz) caster sugar

60 g (2¼ oz) unsalted butter, at room temperature

2 eggs, at room temperature

30 g (1¼ oz) candied peel

grated rind of
1 unwaxed organic orange

grated rind of
1 unwaxed organic lemon

6 tablespoons Italian oo flour

½ tablespoons baking powder

½ teaspoon sea salt

500 g (1 lb) fresh ricotta

unsalted butter, for greasing

Ricotta cheese is often included in cakes and puddings in central and southern Italy. If you can, use ewe milk ricotta, which is tastier than cow's milk cheese.

1 Put the orange water in a small saucepan and heat it. Soak the sultanas in it for about 20 minutes.

2 Set aside 1 tablespoon of the sugar. Put the rest of the sugar in a bowl and add the eggs, one at the time, beating well after each addition until the mixture is pale and creamy. Add the candied peel, lemon and orange rind, flour, baking powder and salt.

3 Press the ricotta through the small disc of a food mill or through a sieve and add to the other ingredients. Fold the ricotta thoroughly into the mixture with a metal spoon. Add the sultanas and orange water and mix again.

4 Generously butter a 20 cm (8 inch) springform cake tin and sprinkle with the reserved sugar to coat the bottom and sides of the tin.

5 Spoon the ricotta mixture into the tin and cook in a preheated oven, 180°C (350°F), Gas Mark 4, for about 1 hour or until the cake has shrunk slightly from the sides of the tin. Leave to cool in the tin and then unmould on to a round dish and decorate as you wish.

Polenta biscuits
Zaleti

MAKES ABOUT
50 BISCUITS

125 g (4 oz) polenta flour

60 g (2¼ oz) Italian 00
flour

¼ teaspoon baking
powder

pinch of sea salt

150 g (5 oz) icing sugar,
sifted

100 g (3½ oz) unsalted
butter, at room
temperature

grated rind of
1 unwaxed organic
lemon

There are two versions of these biscuits, known as Zaleti*, one from Padua, where they contain sultanas and the other, this one, from Bologna. In Italy they are often dipped in grappa, but they are equally delicious with ice cream or zabaglione.*

1 Put the polenta, flour, baking powder and salt on the work surface and mix well. Make a mound with a well in the centre and put the sugar, butter and lemon rind into it. Mix in the flour from the walls of the well and knead quickly to form a ball.

2 Divide the dough into 2 pieces, wrap them in clingfilm and put them in the refrigerator for at least 1 hour.

3 Unwrap one of the balls and roll it out to about 5 mm (¼ inch) thick. Use a round, 5 cm (2 inch) biscuit cutter to cut out as many discs as you can and transfer them to a baking sheet. Press the leftover dough together and cut out more discs. Transfer the sheet to a preheated oven, 180°C (350°F), Gas Mark 4, and cook for about 7 minutes or until the biscuits are deep gold in colour.

4 While the first batch is cooking, roll out the second ball of dough and proceed as before.

5 When the biscuits are cooked place them on a metal rack to cool. When they are cold store them in an airtight tin.

Hazelnut biscuits
Brutti ma buoni

MAKES ABOUT
50 BISCUITS
4 egg whites
250 g (8 oz) caster sugar
250 g (8 oz) hazelnuts,
  lightly toasted and
  coarsely ground

The Italian name of this recipe, Brutti ma buoni, *means 'ugly but good'. They are traditional biscuits from Piedmont and are often served with Zabaglione (see pages 144–5).*

1 Put the egg whites into a perfectly clean bowl and whisk until they form stiff peaks.

2 Add the sugar a spoonful at a time, beating constantly, and then stir in the hazelnuts.

3 Transfer the mixture to a heatproof bowl and place the bowl over a saucepan half-full of hot, but not boiling, water. Cook the mixture, stirring constantly, over the hot water for 15 minutes. The mixture will become very thick and smaller in volume.

4 Line 2 baking sheets with nonstick baking paper and use a teaspoon to spoon small heaps of the mixture on the sheets.

5 Place the sheets in a preheated oven, 160°C (325°F), Gas Mark 3, for 30–40 minutes until the biscuits are pale golden. Put the biscuits on wire racks and, when cold, store in an airtight tin.

Black rice pudding
Riso nero

SERVES 6

600 ml (1 pint) full-fat milk

75 g (3 oz) Italian rice, preferably Vialone Nano

100 g (3½ oz) sugar

100 g (3½ oz) almonds, blanched and lightly toasted

pinch of sea salt

1 stick of cinnamon

150 ml (¼ pint) black coffee

40 g (1½ oz) plain dark chocolate, flaked or grated

grated rind of 1 unwaxed organic orange

15 g (½ oz) unsalted butter

150 ml (¼ pint) whipping cream

This is one of the few rice dishes to originate from Sicily. I serve it with whipping cream, which is not done in its homeland.

1 Put the milk, rice, sugar, almonds, salt, cinnamon and coffee in a heavy-based saucepan. Bring to the boil and simmer, stirring frequently, over a low heat for about 1 hour or until the rice is soft. (If you use a flame diffuser you do not need to stir frequently, but take care because the milky rice tends to stick to the bottom of the pan.)

2 Remove the pan from the heat and mix in the chocolate and orange rind. Remove the cinnamon stick.

3 Grease a 1 litre (1¾ pint) pudding basin with the butter. Spoon in the rice mixture and leave to cool. When it is cold, cover with clingfilm and put in the refrigerator to chill.

4 Use a palette knife to loosen the pudding all round the basin and turn it out on to a round serving dish. Whip the cream and spread it all over the dome just before serving.

Wild cherry jam tart
Crostata di amarene

SERVES 6

PASTRY

225 g (7½ oz) Italian oo flour

½ teaspoon sea salt

100 g (3½ oz) icing sugar, sieved

grated rind of ½ unwaxed organic lemon

125 g (4 oz) unsalted butter

2 eggs

1 egg yolk

FILLING

50 g (2 oz) ground almonds

350 g (11½ oz) cherry or damson jam

2 tablespoons organic lemon juice

In Italy wild cherry jam is used for this tart because of its intense, yet slightly sour, flavour. You can use morello cherry or damson jam.

1 Make the pastry. Make a mound of the flour on the work surface and mix in the salt, sugar and lemon rind. Rub in the butter, add the eggs and knead as quickly as you can to form a ball. Alternatively, make the dough in a food processor. Wrap the dough in clingfilm and leave to rest for 30 minutes.

2 Butter a loose-bottomed 23 cm (9 inch) tart tin and sprinkle with some flour, shaking off the excess.

3 Set aside about one-third of the dough and roll out the remainder to make a circle large enough to cover the base of the tin and the edge. Press the dough firmly into the tin and sprinkle with the ground almonds.

4 Put the jam in a bowl and mix with the lemon juice. Use a wet spatula to spread the jam all over ground almonds.

5 Roll out the remaining dough and use a pastry wheel to cut strips about 2 cm (¾ inch) wide. Arrange the strips over the jam to form a lattice that covers the surface of the tart. (Don't worry if you have to join some of the strips. When they are cooked, the joints won't show.)

6 Place the tin in a preheated oven, 200°C (400°F), Gas Mark 6, and bake for 10 minutes. Reduce the temperature to 180°C (350°F), Gas Mark 4, and bake for a further 15–20 minutes until the pastry is golden. Remove the tart from the tin and put it on a wire rack to cool.

Rice cake with almonds and sultanas
Torta di riso

SERVES 8

4 tablespoons sultanas

4 tablespoons dark rum

750 ml (1¼ pints) full-fat milk

175 g (6 oz) caster sugar

strip of unwaxed organic lemon rind, yellow part only

piece of vanilla pod, 2.5 cm (1 inch) long

piece of cinnamon stick, 5 cm (2 inches) long

150 g (5 oz) Italian rice, preferably Arborio

150 g (5 oz) almonds, blanched and peeled

4 eggs, separated

grated rind of ½ unwaxed organic lemon

butter, for greasing

dried breadcrumbs, for the tin

icing sugar

sea salt

Rice cakes of various kinds are popular all over central Italy, and this is one of the many versions.

1 Put the sultanas in a bowl and pour over the rum. Set aside.

2 Meanwhile, put the milk, 30 g (1¼ oz) of the sugar, the lemon rind, vanilla pod, cinnamon stick and a pinch of salt in a saucepan and bring to the boil. Add the rice and stir well with a wooden spoon. Cook, uncovered, over a low heat for about 35 minutes, stirring frequently, until the rice has absorbed the milk and is soft and gluey. Set aside to cool.

3 Spread the almonds on a baking sheet and toast them in a preheated oven, 180°C (350°F), Gas Mark 4, for about 10 minutes or until they are quite brown. Shake the sheet occasionally to prevent them from burning. Allow them to cool a little, then chop them coarsely. Leave the oven on.

4 Remove the lemon rind, vanilla pod and cinnamon stick from the rice and spoon the rice into a mixing bowl. (Wash and dry the vanilla pod so that you can use it again.) Incorporate 1 egg yolk at a time into the rice, mixing well after each addition. Add the remaining sugar, the almonds, the sultanas with the rum and the grated lemon rind and mix everything together thoroughly.

5 Whisk the egg whites until they are stiff, then fold them gently into the rice mixture.

6 Butter a 20 cm (8 inch) springform cake tin. Line the bottom with nonstick baking paper and butter the paper. Sprinkle all over with breadcrumbs to coat evenly and shake out the excess crumbs.

7 Spoon the rice mixture into the tin and bake in the oven (still at the same temperature) for 45–60 minutes or until a thin skewer or a wooden cocktail stick inserted in the middle of the cake comes out just moist. This is a moist cake, even when well cooked.

8 Leave the cake in the tin to cool, then turn it out on to a dish. Leave for at least 24 hours, then sprinkle generously with icing sugar before serving.

Index

Acknowledgements

Executive Editor: Eleanor Maxfield
Senior Editor: Lisa John
Creative Director: Tracy Killick
Design concept: Smith & Gilmour
Designer: Grade Design
Photographer: Noel Murphy
Home Economist: Sue Henderson
Home Economist's Assistants: Rachel Wood and Ramona Andrews
Stylist: Wei Tang
Senior Production Controller: Amanda Mackie